STRIPPED

D1485221

MARNIE SIMPSON

Stripped Bare

arrow books

1 3 5 7 9 10 8 6 4 2

Arrow Books
20 Vauxhall Bridge Road
London SW1V 2SA

Arrow Books is part of the Penguin Random House group of companies
whose addresses can be found at global.penguinrandomhouse.com.

Penguin
Random House
UK

First published in Great Britain by Century in 2017
Published by Arrow Books in 2018

www.penguin.co.uk

A CIP catalogue record for this book is available
from the British Library.

ISBN 9781784758417

Typeset in 10.68/15.55 pt Melior LT Std by Jouve (UK), Milton Keynes
Printed and bound in Great Britain by Clays Ltd, St Ives plc

Penguin Random House is committed to a sustainable future
for our business, our readers and our planet. This book is made
from Forest Stewardship Council® certified paper.

MIX
Paper from
responsible sources
FSC® C018179

For Mam – my best friend, my rock, my soulmate.

CONTENTS

ACKNOWLEDGEMENTS

First of all I'd like to thank all my friendships and relationships. Without all of them, I wouldn't have learned all the lessons I have, which have ultimately determined the person I've become. Whether it's been good or bad I've learned so much in my life and I will continue to.

I'd like to thank my Nana and Grandad for teaching me how to be the best version of myself, and for being the best role models in my life. I also want to thank my Mam for being the best Mam I could ever ask for, my best friend, my rock and my soul mate. I wouldn't be where I am today if it wasn't for you, so I dedicate this book to you – you truly are an amazing woman.

And also a big shout out to both my fathers; Daddy brat for coming into my Mam's life and making her happy and always helping me out with hugs and advice, and my Dad for being a soldier no matter how bad the struggles are and always remaining a kind soul.

And last, but not least, I need to thank all of the people from Century and Penguin Random House UK for all of their hard work, and for giving me the opportunity to write my autobiography – in particular I'd like to thank Ajda for going the extra mile. Thank you to David Riding from MBA for believing in me and the project. There wouldn't be a book if it wasn't for everyone at MTV and Lime, in particular Kerry, Craig, Lauren and Jake. Thank you to Helena Drakakis for helping me to tell my story and being so patient and understanding along the way. I'd also like to thank Emma, Craig and Molly from my management, Unleashed PR, for all their hard work.

PHOTOGRAPHIC ACKNOWLEDGEMENTS

Second Plate Section

Page 3 – 'Sophie wasn't happy . . .' [Bottom] – © Sophie Kasaei

Page 5 – 'Chloe Goodman and me' – © Xposure Photos

Page 6 – 'Me and my manager, Craig . . .' – © Craig Johnson-
        Pass

Page 7 – '*Geordie Shore*, has opened doors . . .' – © Stacey Clarke
        – 'Coming out was hard . . .' – © Lezli & Rose/DIVA

All other photographs are author's own.

Every reasonable effort has been made to contact all copyright
holders, but if there are any errors or omissions, we will insert
the appropriate acknowledgement in subsequent printings of
this book.

INTRODUCTION

How do I start my book? It's been buzzing round my brain non-stop. I'm prone to thinking a lot, me. It may come as a surprise, but I'm much more than a pretty face!

I'm Marnie, by the way. If you're a fan of the MTV show *Geordie Shore*, you'll know who I am – I'm twenty-five years old and I'm the boy-crazy nutbag who loves to have a laugh. You may have scrolled over me online too, or seen me in the papers: at times on the red carpet looking like a million dollars; at others sprawled on a pavement looking mortal and having a mega meltdown! My ex-boyfriend Lewis Bloor probably caused a few of them!

I'm guessing you've got an opinion of me. It might be good or bad, but I think you should never judge a book by its cover. I try not to (OK, I admit, I've not actually read many books!), but it's one of the reasons I wanted to write my own story. And I hope that's why you wanted to read it! There's a lot more to me than the lass in the *Sun* or on my Twitter or Instagram feeds.

But, as I said, I've been thinking, so I've decided to start this book with me dog, Elvis. I know, I know, my book's supposed to be about me! But Elvis is very special in my life. I bought him with my first ever pay cheque from *Geordie Shore*, and I named him Elvis because I love all those old glam 1950s singers and movie stars. I had thought about naming him after the bad boy American actor James Dean, but 'James Dean the dog', doesn't have a good ring to it. So it's Elvis – he's a real heartbreaker, though me mam definitely wouldn't agree! Elvis is dead naughty.

Don't ask me what breed he is, because I've no idea. The random I bought him off swore to me that he was a chihuahua – but he definitely lied to us! I reckon he's part Jack Russell, part sausage dog with a bit of bulldog thrown in. He's so fat he looks like a barrel with legs. No joke; his legs are almost breaking under his weight – probably because Mam feeds him Big Mac meals! But I love him.

The day I bought him, I'd travelled to this rough neighbourhood near where I'm from in South Shields on Tyneside. He was sat on his own in the corner. I swear he was the ugliest dog of the litter. I thought no one would ever pick him. But he looked at me with these big grey eyes, and when I edged forward to stroke him, he ran over and jumped up on my lap. I adored him from that moment on, even though he bites everyone except me, and he loves eating my knickers. Seriously! Not me mam's, just mine! He doesn't even care if they're dirty or clean. I find him with his head in my laundry basket and, no joke, he'll rip out the crotch with his teeth and chew it. So many of my knickers are crotchless, and all because I picked Elvis.

If you're wondering, this is a theme in my life because my last year's Christmas tree was picked in exactly the same way. I'd just moved to London and I was living in my first flat in the north-east of the city, and me mam, Sharon, and stepdad, Eric, were due to spend Christmas with me and my boyfriend Lewis's family. I wanted our place to look homely and welcoming so we went to this massive store filled with gorgeous trees – snow white fir trees and big bushy pines, all decorated with sparkly lights and bows and baubles. Lewis kept pointing to them and saying, 'Let's get this one!' But, no. My eyes were drawn to the tree in the corner, all lanky and crooked and skinny and alone. The runt. I felt sorry for it!

That's exactly what I'm like. I hate it when someone or something is left out.

I think, deep down, they remind me of me. For as long as I can remember I've always been a bit of a loner. Mam says that too, only she calls me a 'character', which I think's a polite way of saying I was *really* weird. It's probably why I took to reality TV like a duck to water – you can't just be normal on TV. I mean, who in the *Geordie Shore* house is? Everyone in the North East is a bit mental anyway, but when you stick them in a house with a load of booze and cameras, it's bound to go off!

Believe it or not, though, growing up I was a shy lass. I didn't do half the drinking or partying I do now, but everyone says I was a bit of a rebel. I'd forgotten some of the things I got up to until I had to remember them all for this book, and I'll let you into a secret: I'm not always proud of myself!

I'm proud of me family, though. Me mam, who I mentioned earlier, is the rock in my life. Her and me stepdad Eric are my support system, alongside me nana and grandad. At times, I've really needed them. And my friends, too – the handful I have from home and now my *Geordie Shore* family. I'm a girl with a crazy head, a big heart and even bigger dreams. If I've made mistakes, I've learned from them. But whatever's happened to me, I can never say that life's been boring. So, here goes, welcome to me book!

CHAPTER 1

FIFTY SHADES OF GREY

Before you get proper excited, this chapter isn't about sex. You'll have to wait until at least Chapter Three for boys, and probably Chapter Ten before my sex life starts getting interesting. I was definitely what you'd call a late bloomer! No, when I'm talking about fifty shades of grey, I'm not talking about silk ties, handcuffs or riding crops. I'm talking about my home town of Stanley. Even though it's a tiny town in County Durham filled with rows of red-brick, terraced houses, it's always looked grey to me. Fifty shades is nowhere near enough – it's fifty shades darker!

You'd think being twelve miles from Newcastle and surrounded by rolling green fields that it would be a brilliant place to grow up, but Stanley was nothing short of crap. It's a dark place. I don't want to slag it off too much because me dad and nana and grandad still live there. They know all about the history of Stanley and the coal mine and the men who used to work in it, but that closed years and years ago, way before I came into the world.

When I was growing up, all I remember about Stanley was that there was nothing to do – not for young people, anyway. No cinema; no swimming pool; there wasn't even a train station, so unless you had a car you couldn't leave. Its main street is a depressing parade of shops – betting shops, bakeries and a Job Centre, and even though her family lived near us, Mam couldn't wait to get out either. It's always been really rough; like a brawler town. At night, you walked down the high street scared you might get your throat slit. Honestly, it was that bad. It's no wonder she was desperate for somewhere better for me to spend my childhood.

Mam gave birth to me in nearby Shotley Bridge Hospital in Consett on 17 January 1992. Me dad, nana and grandad were all with her when I popped out weighing 6lb 1oz. They never married, but Mam and Dad were definitely an item when I was born. It's obvious from the pictures they fancied each other, but I don't think they lasted too long after that. Whenever I ask Mam, she's a bit vague on the subject, although she says they were dead in love with each other in the five years they were together. But me dad's had problems in his life. He's had demons to fight.

In photos, me dad is dead good-looking with fairish hair and piercing blue eyes. Me mam also looks fresh-faced with a scraped back ponytail and big, gold, hoop earrings. I don't think she's changed much and, to me, Mam always looks amazing. They are both quite fair, though, so I do always wonder, 'Where the hell did I come from?'

I didn't see much of me dad after they split, but I've always liked that when I was born me mam and dad were in love. Even when they weren't together, I don't remember any anger or bitterness between them. If I think about it now, I'm glad I never got used to them being together or got to rely on me dad. If I had, I reckon them splitting up would have been 100 times worse. As it was, I never missed what I never had, and whenever me dad was around he was always lovely with me. It's just that he wasn't around too much.

As a baby, I have zero memories of him living with us, but he must have done because three days after I was born he properly saved my life.

Before I tell you this story, I have to tell you something about Mam. She'll kill me for saying this, but she's not good in a crisis. She's so erratic and she gets into a right panic. Most of the time, she won't deal with anything. Instead, she'd rather run from a room screaming. Mice, spiders, filling out official forms – anything like that and she's off the scale of mental! Don't get me wrong. I'm very close to me mam. We're a team. But she's a nightmare stress-head at times and the worst thing is, I've learned it all from her!

On this occasion, she'd not long brought me home from hospital, and she was bathing me upstairs when suddenly I stopped breathing. My cheeks started to turn blue, then purple and my eyes began rolling backwards. Mam just froze – she had no idea what to do next! Instead of trying to resuscitate me, she started screaming at the top of her voice. Thanks loads, Mam! If it hadn't been for me dad legging it upstairs, yanking me from the water, dangling me upside down by my legs and hitting me hard on the back, I probably wouldn't be here. Apparently, the mucus hadn't cleared from my throat properly after I'd been born and it was stopping me from taking in air. Instead of coughing it up, I'd started choking. Soon, I was back on the maternity ward and under close supervision for another two weeks.

Mam's never been wealthy, but I was spoiled with love. Apart from her being useless in a disaster, I always felt like Mam would die for us. Other than the odd cleaning job, she never worked. She always struggled to find a job, so it's not like I ever had nice outfits or lots of material things growing up. But unlike other members of my family, Mam and I had something special between us, and that was enough.

Mam has an older sister, Julie, who has a daughter, Mischa. They used to live in Stanley, too. Then there's Mam's younger sister, Eunice, who is mam to my cousin Sophie Kasaei, who became the first member of our family to star in *Geordie Shore*. They live in South Shields, which is half an hour from Stanley, and although Sophie grew up rich by comparison and she always visited us dressed so lovely, I noticed there was never the same bond between her and her mam as there was between me and mine. It was the same with Julie and Mischa so I always felt very lucky to have that strong relationship. It felt like us against the world.

Even friends who are close to their mams comment on it. If they've watched the way we interact with each other they say it's very unique, like we're best friends, or telepathic. It's probably because I've spent most of my life with her.

The house she brought me home from hospital to was right next to what became my primary school, but I don't remember anything about it. I must have been around four when we moved to a bigger place on Wear Road. It was soooooo old fashioned! Downstairs had bare wooden floors and big, ugly blue settees and there was even a coal fire in the living room. Every week the coal merchant used to deliver this huge sack of dirty black coal off the back of his lorry – proper dark ages!

Mam was convinced the house was haunted. There was an eeriness about it – like something or somebody was always there. The minute you opened the front door, you shivered. That's why she and I always used to sleep together. Well . . . it's not the only reason. I loved sleeping with Mam because it meant neither of us were alone. It was always me and her cuddled up together in her double bed – even though my own room was only a few steps across the hallway. It's hard to believe I never slept under my own duvet until I started secondary school.

Mam kept this story from me for ages because she didn't want to scare me, but one night she swears she saw a ghost. It was in the early hours of the morning and she opened her eyes to find a knight standing over her. No joke. A knight, like from medieval times! Aside from his basin haircut, he was dressed head to toe in silver armour and chain mail. She was so terrified, she sat bolt upright and pinned herself against the back wall. She says the image of him is still imprinted on her brain because he stared right through her before silently turning and walking out of the room. Thank God I never saw him. I would have been properly traumatised!

One of the other reasons I hated my own room was

it was really cluttered. Ask anyone in the *Geordie Shore* house – I'm a total hoarder and a skanky mare too! Despite being a right tomboy, my room was wall-to-wall pink: pink carpet, pink wallpaper and a single bed with a pink veil suspended from the ceiling and draped around it. I was always sure I was a boy in another life, but I'm starting to think I was a bit of a princess too. I still love the colour pink, though I've *never* been girlie!

I hardly spent any time in that room even though it had a TV and all my stuff in it. I preferred my room at Nana and Grandad's. Compared to ours, their house was so homely and cosy. Betty and Malcolm are me dad's parents and I loved staying with them. Unlike Mam's family, they've always been very stable and grounded and they're the people I've looked up to in life. They were my one piece of normality.

It's awful for Mam to hear that, and I don't like saying it in front of her because I know she did her best for us and she has so much love for me. But Nana and Grandad could look after me in ways Mam couldn't. For example, Mam's never been able to drive, so there were times when I'd watch my friends being picked up from school by their parents and the rain would be pouring from the skies and I'd have to walk through Stanley's grey streets and get the bus home on my own. But on the days when Nana came, the sun shone. When I knew she was picking us up,

I'd always run through the school gates looking out for her waiting car and her horn-rimmed glasses peering over the steering wheel. I'd jump up in the front seat, give her a big kiss and she'd take me to hers for tea.

Every mealtime in that house was an occasion. Setting the table and putting the drinks out was my job, and Nana and Grandad cooked all my favourite dishes. One of these was egg fried rice with peppers, like a stir fry, and Nana would make the best pease pudding. *Hold on. Rewind!* You're probably thinking, what the hell is pease pudding? If you've never been to the North East, you definitely won't have tasted it, so let me translate. It's made from boiled split peas and onions and herbs. Sounds disgusting, doesn't it? But it isn't. Not the way me nana makes it, anyway! Occasionally we'd also get a Chinese takeaway on a Saturday night and then cuddle up on the sofa to watch *Who Wants to Be a Millionaire?* or *X Factor.*

Nana and Grandad weren't exactly millionaires, but by comparison, I suppose Mam was just getting by. With her, I had a funny routine that was never, ever predictable. The only days Mam did take me or pick me up from school were the days Lenny could drive us. But Lenny wasn't even family! He was our neighbour. He was hilarious and we all loved him. He was this old, thin, frail man with a tiny sprout of strawberry blonde hair he used to try to comb over his whole head. He could barely walk, yet he'd offer to go on errands for her and if Mam needed anything, he'd be round like a shot and he'd always take her to Asda to do her shopping, which was a good ten minutes from where we lived. I was so gutted a few years ago when I found out Lenny had died. He was so soft-natured and kind and, without him, Mam would never have been able to do half the things she did with me. It's only now I've passed my driving test I realise how hard it must have been for her to bring me up on her own with no money and no transport.

Being at Nana's house was different, though. Whereas Mam's house had wooden floors, Nana's had big, thick carpets that you could sink your toes into. It had three bedrooms and two sitting rooms and Grandad spent ages putting decking in the back garden and tending to all the plants and flowers. He's a dead keen gardener and he even has birdhouses dotted around the trees. All my toys were in my bedroom there, and although every time Mam came to pick me up I was desperate to see her, I'd cry because I never wanted to leave.

Another good thing about me being there was that me dad used to visit, although that didn't happen every week. In the early days, he was away working. He worked on construction sites and I'm convinced he helped build the Alton Towers theme park. He definitely built those big out-of-town supermarkets all around the country. As far as I was concerned, he probably built the Empire State Building, too, because I used to think he was this big, tough hero. But the reality was he worked so hard to blot everything out. Not that I ever saw him upset, but I would often overhear Nana and Grandad talking, or me mam and her sisters whispering about him. Children just know, don't they? Even if they don't fully understand. In lots of ways, they tried to shield his problems from me. Thank God Dad's always been good to me. That's probably the reason why Mam and him never had a volatile relationship after they separated. The way I would describe him is that he bottles everything up, like lots of men, I guess. But over the years I always make the effort to reconnect with him. One day he might not be here. I've only got now.

Not long after Mam and I moved to the haunted house, he married another woman. Again, Mam was dead supportive of him and his new relationship. That's just what she's like. As for me, it didn't bother me that Dad had a new family either, but as I've got older, I've realised perhaps it did bother me more than I ever let on. Deep down, I felt disappointed; not bitter, not angry, just disappointed.

Six years after I was born, they had their first son, Ben, and he was followed four years later by his brother, Daniel. We used to play together if they came round to Nana's, but when they were picked up, I was on my own again. If they were going out, or if they ever went on holiday, I wasn't included. Unbelievably, I didn't go on holiday with me dad until I was seventeen (and that's a whole different story!), but at the time, I didn't understand. I understand it more now. I've got mates who have had one child and gone on to have kids with new partners. It's a complicated situation, but I do feel me dad went along just to keep the peace.

If I'm being brutally honest, I found being around Dad awkward. We've never had the same relationship that me and Mam have and it felt a bit distant. Maybe it sounds ridiculous, but every time he left Nana's I'd always run up, throw my arms around him and say, 'Love you', but I sensed he never wanted to give me too much attention.

The worst time was when he turned up at Nana's with a new tattoo. I didn't notice it until we were all sat round the table, but in the design there were only three names not four. My heart sank. It felt like I'd been wounded. 'What about me?' I kept thinking. Was I not part of his family? Little things like that meant the connection between us got weaker, but I would never have been brave enough to tell him he'd upset me. Instead, I kept it all inside. Maybe I even put my guard up, just to stop myself from feeling hurt by him. If I got close to him, he might always let me down. At the ripe old age of twenty-five, I'm beginning to realise

I never really face how I feel. A bit like him; I blot everything out.

Whenever I did go on holiday, it was with Nana and Grandad. Bless them, they were always trying to make up for me dad. Most years we'd go away in the caravan, travelling up and down the country to all the holiday sites. Mam never came with us, which I did feel sad about, but I was the centre of their universe for two weeks every summer.

By far the most exciting trip was when I was five and they took me to Florida. Because I was so tiny, I only have vague memories of that holiday, but fortunately me grandad made several home videos to remind me. Thanks, Grandad! There's one very, very cute video of me waking up in our hotel, rubbing my eyes and squinting at the morning sunshine. The most embarrassing one is of me sat in the hotel room attempting to cram a monster burger in my mouth. It's almost the size of me head! 'You've got a bigger mouth than Jaws!' Grandad is laughing at me. Obviously nothing's changed! It's safe to say that film has never been shown to any of my boyfriends!

It's true, though; as a child I always loved my food. And I swear that's because of Nana and Grandad. I loved sweets, too. What kid doesn't? But as Mam lived opposite a sweet shop, I used to get a £2 mix-up every day. It was proper olde worlde – a shelf groaning with cola bottles, sugary jellies, sherbets and liquorice allsorts. I was so greedy, it's no wonder I was the chubbiest child on the planet.

Anyway, back in Florida, it was sweltering hot. Coming from Tyneside, it's not like we ever knew what sunshine was! We went to the MGM Studios and I remember being so small and walking into this place where everything seemed so big. In Universal Studios, too, there were attractions from the cartoons I loved like *Scooby-Doo* and props from films like *Jurassic Park*. Walt Disney's Magic Kingdom seemed like another world – so different to anything I'd ever seen before – and when I saw all the colours of the Cinderella Castle my eyes almost popped out my head! Yogi Bear and Mickey and Minnie Mouse are all in my photos, and when we drove on the three-lane highways, I'd just stare out of the window, wide-eyed and smiling, watching everything go by. It was as if I'd died and gone to heaven. It's funny to think that now I've travelled the world with *Geordie Shore*, but back then, my life was so small I'd never even left the country!

The minute we got back to Stanley, I couldn't wait to tell Mam. After a long flight, I jumped from the car and ran across the front garden to hug her. We watched the home videos together and I probably didn't notice it at the time, but Mam got upset seeing them. We've talked about it since and she says, 'I wish I could have done that for you, Marnie.' If ever I hear her talk like that I say, 'Mam, you spoiled me with love.' All the money in the world can't buy me that.

CHAPTER 2

MAMA BEAR

Mam's house was the house with no rules. I don't remember a proper bedtime or mealtime, or ever being grounded. Some people might say that's terrible parenting, but Mam wasn't a terrible parent. She just wasn't strict. When I was younger she used to let me get away with murder, but I think that had a good effect on me when I was a teenager. I was probably better-behaved because she didn't suffocate me with rules like my friends' mams and dads.

Grandad, on the other hand, was the disciplinarian in our family. It was his way or the highway, and we've ended up having some blazing rows over the years. He has my interests at heart, but sometimes he'd grief me constantly and it was *waaayyy* too much.

Having said that, Mam did smack my bum a few times, and we did argue, but I knew she was always there for us in the end.

One time, after I'd started at Shield Row Primary School, I was picked to be a fairy in the school play. The performance was in the afternoon and Mam was supposed to take me early so I could get ready and she could watch the show. But no, Marnie decided to have a pure radge moment (in Geordie-land, that's a tantrum) and Lenny ended up taking me without her. What the fuss was about, I've no idea, because we often argued over stupid things. I cried all the way to school and once I'd got my costume on, I found a spot backstage and watched from behind the curtain as all the other mams and dads trickled into the hall and took their seats. I started to get dead scared. I couldn't see Mam anywhere. I was so desperate to catch eyes with her and make everything OK, but she didn't appear. It wasn't until the performance started and I was up on stage that I clocked her sitting at the back of the hall, watching my every move. That was all I needed. From that day on, I knew she would never let us down.

Mam was my hero, too. No joke – she once brought my hamster back from the dead. *She did!* We still talk about it to this day. He was called Mr Jingles after the mouse in the film *The Green Mile* starring Tom Hanks. Every day when I came home from school, I would rush to take him out of his cage and play with him. But there was one time I reached in and he was on his back with his feet in the air. His eyes were tight shut and he wasn't breathing. I was devastated. 'He's dead, Mam,' I kept crying. She picked him up, sat on the sofa, placed him on her knee and rubbed his belly very gently. She rubbed and rubbed for two whole hours until slowly his feet started moving and his eyes began flickering, and the more she rubbed the more he came back to life. Amazingly, he lasted for another six months, and after that I said she had healing hands. I swear our house was a magnet for animals. We had a cat called Buffy and one called Belle. Mam said we couldn't afford to keep Buffy so we took her to a shelter at Shotley Bridge, which was a couple of miles away. But after a few days, a cat rushed through our cat flap and began eating from Buffy's food tray. She was this raggier version of Buffy, and I was convinced she'd escaped because she was missing us so much.

I loved my first school, but as I mentioned, I was a bit of a loner. According to Mam, I was dead melodramatic too – always thinking about life and death and the universe and overthinking everything! It's not like I was ever christened, but apparently I talked a lot about God and heaven, and spirituality. I don't think I've changed much! But that's not normal, is it?

My family described me as an 'old head on young shoulders'. I was very mature in some ways, but not in others. I remember me Auntie Julie once saying she would sit and tell me her problems. Halfway through, she'd stop, wake up and think, 'Why the hell am I telling an eight-year-old about me life?'

I always wanted to look after Mam. Because she never had any money, I dreamed of winning the lottery or finding the thickest wodge of banknotes and that would be me and Mam's ticket out of Stanley.

That wish almost came true! Well, sort of . . . I must have been snooping around at Nana and Grandad's, pulling out every drawer to see what I could find and – *result!* – I struck gold. In the room they used as an office, in an envelope tucked into one of the drawers was a stack of ten- and twenty-pound notes. I reckon there was around £500 there, not that I counted it. I was just so happy to have found any money. I listened out for footsteps and quickly shoved the envelope in my jeans pocket.

That weekend I was so excited to get home because I was bursting to give the envelope to Mam.

'It's a present from Nana and Grandad,' I told her, holding out the envelope with a massive grin on my face. Deep down, I knew they probably couldn't afford to give her £500, but who cared? I was buzzing that I was saving Mam!

She took it, but she called Nana straight away,

which turned out to be the fatal flaw in my otherwise flawless plan . . .

'Thanks so much for the money, Betty,' I could hear her saying.

'What money?' Nana must have replied, because Mam bolted round and stared at me with daggers. I felt so ashamed. As the conversation went on, it became clear that Nana had no idea what Mam was banging on about and that I'd stolen the money. Aside from being in the shit, I remember feeling gutted I couldn't help Mam and we'd be stuck in Stanley forever.

What I didn't realise is that on the weekends when I was away at Nana's, Mam wasn't always stuck indoors by herself. Seriously, at one point I even thought she was a lesbian and she wasn't interested in men at all because, other than me dad, Mam never really had any boyfriends. Now she's hinted she did have a few flings over the years, it's just she never did anything with men when I was at home. In fact, there's only one man who I can remember. He worked at the local Netto supermarket, but I've no idea what his name was. All I remember was his big, shiny, baldy head. One time they were kissing in her room and me and me cousin Mischa crept in under the bed. We were silent at first, but we couldn't stop nudging each other and soon we started sniggering and giggling so loudly that Mam heard, leaped out of bed and dragged us out. Mam won't thank me for telling that story!

Most of the time, I was what you'd call 'a bit special'. But Mam encouraged it! We loved watching films together, and because she was never overly bothered about school, if I wanted a day off she'd peel back the duvet and gesture for me to hop back into bed and say, 'Come on, pet. Let's watch a film.' We'd get sweets and ice cream and stay there for the whole day watching movies. None of my friends ever got to do that, so it was a treat and it felt like my time with her.

Admittedly, I did take some of the films a bit seriously. A week after we watched the film *Cast Away*, also starring Tom Hanks, I became obsessed with balls! There's a sequence in the film where his character, Chuck Noland, who's stranded on a desert island after a plane crash, injures his hand and draws this face on a volleyball with his own blood. He's so lonely that he actually believes it's a real person and starts talking to it! After seeing this, I begged Mam to get me a ball and the minute I got it home, I drew a huge round face on it in red pen. I even tried to put hair on it! Mine wasn't a volleyball, though, it was a football and it became my new best friend. I'd be upstairs having conversations with it all the time.

'Who are you talking to, Marnie?' Mam used to creep up the stairs and shout.

'No one, Mam,' I'd tell her. But I'd even called the ball Mr Wilson, just like Chuck Noland had. Now that's definitely not normal, is it?

My other imaginary friend was called Chantelle, which is weird because I was later to live in the *Geordie Shore* house with Chantelle Connelly who joined in series twelve, and I can't stand the girl. More about her later – there's a part of me that wishes she was imaginary, too!

Another film I adored was *Titanic*. It must have come out when I was around five and Mam rented it from the video shop. Maybe it was because I'd always felt like an ugly duckling, but I wanted to be Kate Winslet in that film so badly. She was dead pretty playing Rose with her gorgeous ringletty red hair and big lips, and you just knew that her and Jack, played by Leonardo DiCaprio, would die for each other. All that year I had pictures cut out from magazines of Leonardo DiCaprio plastered across my school jotters next to large love hearts that I'd coloured in. I was obsessed! That last scene when Rose is floating on the raft and Jack is clinging to it in the icy cold Atlantic always made me bawl. I replayed it over and over. I wanted all the attention that Jack gave her. Maybe I even wanted a boy to die for me because he loved me so much. I might have taken it a bit far, though, when I stripped naked and made me cousin Sophie draw me, just like Jack did to Rose in the film. I'd climb on

Mam's settee with nothing on but a pound-shop necklace, and repeat the line in the film, 'Draw me like one of your French girls,' in this sexy voice. I was an embarrassing sucker for love even back then, always wishing I'd be swept off my feet, just like in the movies.

There were other times when I'd really want to watch a film, but Mam wouldn't let me because it had naughty bits in it. Apparently, I was way too young. *Boring!* When I was eight, she hired the film *Cruel Intentions*, which was set in New York and followed these wealthy teenagers who all fall in love with each other. It's dead steamy and the hottest sex scene is between actors Reese Witherspoon and Ryan Phillippe. Every time I begged Mam to put it on she said, 'No way.' So I thought up a cunning plan. I waited until she wasn't looking and swapped the tape for my *Beauty and the Beast* video. Whenever I heard her coming upstairs to my room *Cruel Intentions* would get switched off, then I'd dive under my duvet and pretend I was reading until she'd gone, then creep back and switch the film on again. I swear she even took *Beauty and the Beast* back to the video shop even though the cover said *Cruel Intentions*!

I was constantly playing games with her and trying to get one up on her. Fooling Mam was always fun, but I'm convinced that deep down I wanted my own way *all* the time.

Once I got to stay off school for weeks because I had this terrible rash on my face. It was red and blotchy and when Mam took me to the doctors he diagnosed me with a virus and ordered me to stay at home until it cleared. Inside, I was doing cartwheels because I'd much rather be at home than school and my plan had worked. I didn't have a virus at all. I'd spent ages in my room painting on the red blotches with lip liner. I kept a straight face, but I couldn't believe I'd got away with it!

Maybe it was because most of my friends lived on Shield Row near my school and our house was further away that I don't recall going to friends' houses or even playing with them. Most of the time I'd just be kicking back in the woods, out walking on my own. Mam was frantic one time and called the police because I'd been out so long. The whole house was in uproar and apparently Mam's stress levels had shot through the roof, but I was oblivious. There were trees to climb and tree houses to build. I was never into make-up or clothes back then. I just threw on any old jeans and a T-shirt. Finding out about the world and having adventures and daring myself to do daft things was all I was interested in.

OK, at times I did take that a bit far, and I roped my cousin Mischa in, too. She was probably the person I hung out with most in Stanley. At the back of our house there was a set of allotments and some garages and I'd spend hours hauling myself up onto roofs and jumping the one-metre gap from garage to garage. They were properly high – probably three times my height! One time Mischa managed to climb onto one garage roof, but then took fright and refused to come down. She was shaking like a jelly and I thought she might be stuck up there forever. Mischa was smaller and not as daring as me. Besides, it was dangerous. Half an hour later, the fire brigade had been called and a drop-dead gorgeous officer dressed in a hard hat and uniform was climbing a ladder and scooping her up in his arms! Oh, the shame!

Despite being a bit of a loner, I liked primary school. Kids can be cruel, though. Like I said, I don't look anything like Mam or Dad. From early on I had jet black hair and dark skin and big bushy eyebrows so I got called names like 'Paki'. I hated that. I used to get loads of racist comments, usually from the harder girls, but I just ignored them.

I also got the piss taken out of me for my clothes. Our uniform was a red jumper with grey trousers or a skirt, but once a year we had no-school-uniform day when we could dress up in whatever we wanted. Because I didn't have many other clothes, Mam sent me to school in my uniform. When all the other girls turned up in their jeans and skirts and glittery tops, I felt so self-conscious. Mam gets defensive whenever I tell that story, but it wasn't her fault. In her heart, she wanted the best for me.

I always had head lice, too, and I could never seem to get rid of them. One teacher even stood me up in front of the class and plucked one from my hair to show everyone. I was that embarrassed I wanted the ground to swallow me up. It's no wonder I hated teachers so much. And another teacher hauled my mam into school because I kept rubbing my vagina up against all the desks. I must have been a very sexual child. I don't think I've changed! Apparently, I used to encourage other girls to do it, too. When they told her, Mam just laughed. The teachers weren't impressed but, seriously, what teacher pulls a parent into school because of that? In fact, the only teacher I loved at primary school was the headmaster, Mr Patterson. He wasn't all about throwing his power around. Instead, he came across as very calm, kind and fair.

Most of the fun I had was outside the classroom, though, and that was also down to me nana. She was always signing me up for hobbies and activities. Every Sunday, I'd go to a pony club at the South Causey Equestrian Centre, which was on the outskirts of Stanley. There's a hotel there, and I still go for a Sunday roast if I'm ever visiting.

All the class would have lunch and then we'd have our lesson, which involved going out on a 'hack' – a posh word for a trot around the woods. Nana used to buy me all the gear. I looked so cute in my little black riding hat and sturdy shoes, and although I started out riding the ponies, I never stopped wishing I was riding the horses. I was dead competitive and always wanted to push myself. There used to be one horse called Thomas who we all wanted to ride and jump with. He was a palomino and his coat was the most gorgeous gold colour and he had a white mane and tail. Thomas was so friendly and he was powerful and fast too. Sadly, although I was riding all through primary school, it was a hobby I never continued.

I stopped after I'd begged me nana to buy me a horse and she refused! In my head, I thought, 'That's it then, if I don't get a horse, I don't want to ride.' I know, I know, this sounds so spoiled. Typical me, always cutting my nose off to spite my face! Meanwhile, I'd taken up trampolining and I *loved* it! Again, Nana got me into it because she'd seen girls doing it at The Louisa Centre – the sports centre in Stanley.

Trampolining literally became my life. I trained five times a week and ended up competing all round the country. Every night I'd walk to the centre with my friends Gemma and Jenelle, who were both at my school, and we'd practise for one or two hours. At first, we started off doing basic bouncing, then star jumps and straddle jumps and tuck jumps and half twists and soon it felt like I was flying. I passed five awards by the age of ten, and by the next year I was taking proper exams with the British Amateur Gymnastics Association and had reached Grade Ten. That involved a front somersault and full twists. Unlike school, this was the one thing I gave my all for.

Years later, after I'd joined *Geordie Shore*, I got to show off my trampolining skills when we pitched up at Infinite Air in Newcastle where they have wall-to-wall Olympic trampolines. Oh my God, if that place had existed when I was learning the sport I'd never have come home! Even though I hadn't trampolined for years, I discovered it's like riding a bike – you never forget how! Chloe Ferry was determined to be the best, but I'd kept it a secret from everyone that I'd almost got to the highest grade of gymnastic trampolining. For a brief moment, after she'd hoisted herself onto the trampolines, I thought she might have some hidden talent too. After all, Chloe is super athletic and she used to be an ice skater. She started when she was six or seven, around the time I began trampolining and, like me, she was competing at a national level when she was in her teens. She was saying, 'I wanna be the best. I wanna be the best.' But I needn't have worried because after a few warm-up jumps she did the shittiest forward flip I've ever seen! Within minutes I was up there rolling and backflipping my head off. Everyone stood there jaws wide open. That was a great feeling! Chloe took one look at me and jokingly mumbled, 'I'm not going to talk to you for a few hours.'

Being back on a trampoline with *Geordie Shore* reminded me so much of the buzz I used to get when I competed. And I used to compete *everywhere*. Every six months or so, if you got through the regional heats, there'd be a competition against all the other clubs around the country. You'd have two routines to complete in front of the judges, depending on what level you were at. I'd be dead nervous, but once I was up there and performing I loved every second of it. And I always had me nana there to support me, good or bad. Trampolining was the one thing in my life I was brilliant at, but that almost came crashing down when Mam eventually got the opportunity to leave Stanley for good.

CHAPTER 3

GOODBYE STANLEY

Ten years before Mam and me eventually got out of Stanley, she'd put her name down on the council waiting list for a place in South Shields. As I mentioned before, my cousin Sophie and her family already lived there and, being on the coast, it was a step up from Stanley. I'm not saying South Shields was full of angels – no way. There were still the same charvers (that's our Geordie word for chavs) but it was bigger. The town had a beach and a fairground and there was loads more to do. And Mam had definitely had enough. Everyone was so depressed in Stanley. There was one night when she'd even come home with two black eyes. I was only eight or nine at the time and I remember being so confused by it.

She'd been out to Stanley's only nightclub, The Clock, with my cousin Carly – Mischa's older sister. It was a complete dive and after it closed for good, the building stood boarded up for ages. On this night, Carly got into some bother with some drunken lads, and Mam stepped in to stick up for her. There were three of them and one of me mam, and one of them screwed up his fist and belted it across Mam's face. She had two massive shiners and she looked awful for days.

The day after the offer came through from the council, we went to see our new home. Compared to the house in Stanley, which was eerie but large, the place being offered to us was a box. It had two bedrooms, but you could barely swing a cat in mine. It was so small, we couldn't even fit my single bed into the room and Grandad ended up having to take the side panels off just to squeeze it in. Nevertheless, Mam jumped at it. It was our ticket out of Stanley and it came at just the right time. I was making the transition from primary school to secondary and it meant she didn't have to take me out of lessons to move. We just packed up what little stuff we had and took it up to South Shields during the holidays.

Our new place wasn't too far from Sandhaven Beach and the Ocean Beach Pleasure Park, which had dodgems, waltzers and a pirate ship, and even a rollercoaster. During the winter, South Shields feels like a bit of a dead-end ghost town, but come spring and summer, families from Newcastle and all over the North East come for the weekend, and tourists pile into town to stay in the chalets or caravans. We were now officially Sand Dancers, which is what you're called if you live in South Shields. That sounds a lot more exotic than South Shields is, though!

Once we'd moved from Stanley, I was so happy. I assumed it was going to be plain sailing, but how wrong was I? Moving school wasn't half as easy as I'd expected. I started Brinkburn School in September 2003. As usual, I kept myself to myself, but there was one girl, Nathalie Pascoe, who hated my guts. She had the reputation of being the hardest girl in the school, and with me being new, she clearly wanted to show me who was boss. Funnily, we'd actually been friends at first, but for reasons I never understood she turned against me. Next thing I knew, she was challenging me to a fight. I was terrified! Not only was she as hard as nails, but she was dead pretty, and I spent the whole run-up to the fight imagining how mortified I was going to be because everyone would be cheering her name when she won!

It was set for after school on the grass verge near where we lived. I'd told Mam all about it. I was shitting myself because I was not a bully and it wasn't in my nature to fight. 'Don't back down, pet. You stand up for yourself.' Wise words from Mam, there.

And I knew I couldn't back down because if I did, Nathalie Pascoe would grief me forever.

After the bell went that day, I walked to the grassy verge. My palms were sweating and my stomach was doing somersaults. I didn't have too many friends, although me cousin Mischa came along for moral support. I would actually pay money to see the replay of this now, but when I saw how big the crowd that had gathered was, I gulped. All I kept thinking about was how much bigger Nathalie Pascoe was than me and how she was going to pummel my brains out.

Pro-boxers had nothing on us. She stood there, staring at me with her lip curled, then . . . *Ding Ding!* The fight started. From round one, I surprised myself! She had long, blonde hair and I managed to wrestle her to the ground and I was yanking at it and scratching and slapping her face. Her arms were flailing around trying to push me off. By now I was sat on her pinning her against the ground and I kept pulling and slapping. *Ding Ding!* Round two and all the chants that had been for her, turned to me. 'Mar-nie! Mar-nie!' the crowd were cheering and yelling. It felt brilliant. She was down for too long and I knew I'd won. I casually got up and said, 'OK. I'm walking away now. See you!' Then I turned and strode away with Mischa running behind. I was looking as cool as a goddam cucumber, but inside my heart was pumping. My words of advice for a first fight at school? Fake it till you make it! No one will ever know you are shitting yourself inside!

When I glanced back at Nathalie Pascoe, she looked embarrassed and dead angry, but that girl never went near me again. Bizarrely, we ended up talking, although she was never in my group of mates. No one from school was, really. I guess it was because Sophie was older than me, and I used to hang round with lots of her friends now we were living close to one another.

Believe it or not, I wasn't big into boys either – although there's always been a bit of me that was boy-crazy – because I was shy and not very confident about how I looked.

The first boy I ever fancied was a next-door neighbour in Stanley called Gavin Hall. I must have been around five. It wasn't like we ever kissed or anything. It was just a crush, but I used to walk with him to school and laugh at *everything* he said. Then there was Jordan Callaghan. I still have him as a friend on Facebook and he was my boyfriend all through primary school. He was this chubby, ginger kid and if I'd progressed on to kissing by then it was probably only a peck on the lips before I ran away!

Another time I got into loads of trouble was when I was still at Shield Row Primary and we went on a week's trip to Thurston in the Lake District to go canoeing. On the first night, I made two of the other girls sneak into the room where all the boys were sleeping. It's not like I had a plan, but whatever we were actually going to do was soon stopped by a teacher wielding a flashlight and us bolting into a wardrobe until we were hauled out and sent back to bed.

They had me down as a rebel from day one. 'Marnie Simpson! What do you think you are doing?' was such a familiar holler from teachers.

I'd be the first to admit I wasn't the brightest spark at school, but to give me my dues, I always tried hard at lessons, even the ones I wasn't interested in. But by the time I got to secondary school, I couldn't give a flying fuck.

Amazingly, I was still trampolining. Thank God, Mam found me a club at the Temple Park Leisure Centre not long after we moved. But even that became difficult, because now I had to compete against all the girls who I used to trampoline with in Stanley. It was horrible! If you've ever seen the film *Bring It On!* you'll know exactly what I'm talking about because one competition I turned up to with me nana was just like it – only that film's about cheerleading not trampolining. It was sooooo bitchy. Every single girl would have murdered their best mate to win that trophy! Again, just like all the competitions, I had two routines to perform in front of the judges, and by then I was doing the craziest moves. I mean batshit crazy! Before you learned any new routine, you'd practise with a rig on, which was basically a hoist on a pulley system. It's because at that level the moves are really dangerous. A coach would guide you through the routine before the harness was removed and you were on your own. No joke, I was somersaulting and twisting and some of it was dead scary! On this day, I could hear all the girls whispering about me as I got up to perform. I was ridiculously nervous because they'd been my mates when I was on their team and now I was this evil enemy!

They needn't have worried because I totally fucked up the first routine, which was the easier of the two. I wasn't prepared enough. I was so nervous my flip ended in chaos. All eyes were on me, and when they knew I'd done badly I could see some of them power-grabbing the air and shouting 'Yessss'. They didn't think I could win, but I took a deep breath and carried on. On my second routine, which was way more difficult, I could see them all leaning back with relief. I know what they were thinking: 'If she can't get the easy moves right then she's got no chance with the hard routine.' Well, I proved everyone wrong – even myself! I totally smashed it! I couldn't believe it! Oh my God, and I won the whole competition! My old friends from Stanley were fuming. They could barely look at me, and I couldn't help strutting around like a peacock, flicking my hair and enjoying the moment. Even to this day, that is such a good memory. And when it came to receiving my trophy, I was buzzing. Remembering all those nerves and all that pain it took for me to get there and then being handed that award was the sweetest feeling. I was bouncing on top of the world for days!

The problem was, if I'd carried on trampolining, it would have taken over my life. When I look at professional gymnasts now, I know how much sacrifice it's taken them to get there, and I was starting to discover boys and going out in South Shields and I didn't want to spend every single night of my life training. It's a shame because I'd got to such a high level, but I clearly remember the night I decided not to go back. Nana was visiting and that evening I stood in front of the telly just before it was time to leave and announced I wanted to go to the park with my friends. Mam and Nana were pleading with me, 'Please don't go, Marnie! Don't give up your trampolining now.' But I was determined. I felt dead sorry for Nana as she'd been the one who had paid for all my lessons, taken me to classes, picked me up and been with me throughout the competitions. I suppose everything happens for a reason and I wanted my friends more than I wanted trampolining. Do I regret stopping? In a way, yes, but I also know I'd have had to have dedicated my life to it. If I'd carried on, I would never have been on *Geordie Shore*, and I wouldn't be doing half of the things I'm doing now. Maybe life wouldn't have been better, but it sure as hell would have been different.

The park I was so desperate to hang out in was West Park at the back of Stanhope Road. There were open grass fields with a bandstand at one end that me, Lorna and Debbie from school used to sit in when it rained. Lorna was in my year at secondary and she was so funny and ditzy. She gossiped away like an old woman. She's an air hostess for Emirates now. Debbie was one year older and the total opposite: lairy and feisty and I've never seen a girl knock back the booze like her. None of us were old enough to buy alcohol or tabs, so we'd wait outside a corner shop until we could beg someone to buy them for us. It always took a while, and loads of people said no, but eventually someone would cave in and we'd walk away with a bottle of Bellabrusco or Lambrini and twenty Lambert & Butlers. Or Debbie would chance it because she always looked older. It's hard to believe, I know, but I wasn't a big drinker back then. In fact, I was scared of alcohol! All the others would be necking loads from the bottle, but I would pretend. I'd pretend to be mortal, too, slurring my words and falling around, but a lot of the time I was actually stone-cold sober. I hated the taste of alcohol, and I didn't get properly pissed until I was around fourteen.

That time, me and Lorna had gone to the park with a couple of boys and I drank a whole two-litre bottle of Bellabrusco. I was sat on the bench and when I tried to stand I couldn't! 'Jeeezzz,' I thought. My head was spinning and my legs felt like they were going to buckle under me. That feeling is now *very* familiar, but not back then! How I got home, I have no idea, but the minute I did I legged it into the toilet and spewed my guts up. That hasn't changed either! I'm still an awful spewer if I've had too much to drink.

I started smoking in secondary school as well but I was never addicted then. Smokers' corner was behind the science lab. I'd take a toke of a tab but never properly inhale and I didn't like the taste much. All my friends were doing it, though, and there was peer pressure to smoke. And it was something to do aside from lessons. Whereas in primary school, teachers had always said I was polite and tried my best, at Brinkburn School I was different. I didn't take anything seriously and I was constantly in trouble. With the exception of science, my school reports were rubbish! In 2004 my head of year said this:

A very mixed and inconsistent report, Marnie, which very much reflects your attitude towards school in general. Until you realise that you are actually here to work and not just to socialise you are never going to reach your true potential. Attendance needs to improve to over 90% and your lateness is unacceptable.

That was me all over – last minute Marnie! At times, I was so bored in class that I'd tell the teacher I needed to go to the bathroom and never come back. Instead, I'd have a wander round the school grounds or up and down the corridors or I'd go and hang out on the bean bags in the computer room. I didn't want to be the bad girl, but the more rebellious I was the more teachers labelled me. Even if a teacher had liked me and taken me under their wing at high school, I don't think I would have listened. I was too stubborn, and I was on report so much it was like a full-time job!

Report was hideous. It made me not want to go to school even more. Usually, I'd get put on report for wearing make-up – even though I didn't even wear that much – or having a bad attitude, or not turning up to lessons. They'd send me to 'The Unit' which was like some kind of awful solitary confinement and I'd have to do all my lessons from there – like proper torture! When I was on report I had to have perfect behaviour for a whole month. And every single day, a teacher had to sign off my report card. *A month?* I could barely last a week and so it became a cycle of me being sent to The Unit, me kicking off, them extending my report and so I was on never-ending detention.

The most amazing thing was that for the whole of secondary school, I never went to PE once! I blagged it – I used my powers of persuasion and the teachers always believed I was ill or I couldn't do it for whatever bullshit excuse I gave them. Swimming was the worst. I mean, who would make teenage girls swim as the first lesson of the day? For starters, I'd spent ages getting ready for school, straightening my hair and putting mascara and lippy on, only to have some teacher tell me I had to put a cozzy on and get soaking wet! I was fuming. I considered it really cheeky. There was no way I was going to spend the rest of the day looking like a drowned rat! The Brinkburn uniform was bad enough – black trousers, black V-neck jumper, a white shirt and a blue tie – without being sweaty and clammy and wet from the indoor pool.

And I'd get fined all the time for truanting. I was gutted because me nana had set up a Halifax account in my name and she used to deposit £20 a week spending money into it for Mam to withdraw for me. But every time Mam got fined for me not attending school, she couldn't pay, and so the fine went up to around £100. In the end, she said I had to flash the cash out of Nana's pocket money. Mam put her foot down on that one and said if I couldn't be arsed going to school, then I had to take the punishment. Did it stop me? No way!

At times, even Mam had to laugh. My first real brush with authority came when me and this lad,

Robbie Smallwood, truanted off school and made our way to Newcastle on the Metro. I'm not even sure I'd ever been to Newcastle on my own before. We loved it – sitting with our feet on the seats and looking out at the Tyne from the bridge at Gateshead. Why in the world I thought this was a good idea, I don't know, but we ended up in this posh restaurant in town. Two twelve-year-olds ordering pizza, drinks and dessert in school hours must have looked ridiculous, but not one person asked us what we were doing. The problem was neither of us had any money to pay the bill, so we legged it! On the count of three both of us grabbed our coats, ran out and straight into the pub next door where we made a crazy dash for the ladies' loos. All the time, we could hear shouting and footsteps behind us. Our chests were thumping but we kept running until we were safely behind the locked cubicle door, whispering to each other to *ssshhh*!

As we were still catching our breath, the door flew open and we could hear the staff scouring the room for us. Someone knocked hard on the door. 'Come on, we know you're in there,' they shouted. We kept silent until we couldn't pretend anymore. We knew it was over. There was nowhere else to go. I sheepishly unlocked the door and we both shuffled out to face the music. By then the police had been called and I'll never forget having to sit in the back seat with Robbie Smallwood, being driven to the station. *I stole a fucking pizza!* Looking back, I hope it was a Hawaiian. I should have got extra pineapple for being such a div! I do remember the dessert being this amazing chocolate fudge cake, though.

The police were proper scary. Loads more scary than Mam, Nana and me grandad put together.

'Name?' one of them barked at me.

'Marnie Simpson,' I mumbled quietly.

'Age?' he continued.

'Twelve.' I'm sure I was fighting back the tears by then.

Mam was called and we had to wait in one of the cells until she and Robbie Smallwood's mam turned up. The look on Mam's face was a picture. At first she was furious. The police made her pay for my meal, but as we were leaving the station, I could hear Mam and Robbie Smallwood's mam giggling behind us. The police probably found it hilarious too, but they had to appear like they wanted to teach us a lesson. 'You're a bloody idiot. You really are an idiot,' Mam kept repeating. 'You've been locked up for stealing a pizza!' She laughed. I had to explain my crime to all my family and friends as well. I was mortified!

CHAPTER 4

BOY-CRAZZZEEE!

My first proper kiss was when I was twelve. Far from being a romantic, private milestone, it was a truly awful experience. Ben Mummet lived on my street and he was in the year above me. All my friends knew I fancied him and I think he fancied me back, but I was so shy and awkward that I would never have done anything without them putting me up to it. 'Are you going to score with Marnie?' they would go on and on at him. Scoring was kissing with tongues, but I'd only ever pecked a guy before. So imagine the scene. It's the school yard at one p.m. Everyone is standing around and Ben and I get pushed together. I lean in, as does he. Our lips touch, but then it all goes *really* pear-shaped. His lips feel all wet and slimy and as our mouths open my teeth start banging against his. And then he sticks his tongue in. Eeeewww! Instead of a nice, soft, slow kiss it's like a salamander darting its tongue in and out – like I'm dinner. So. Did. Not. Want. That. All of a sudden, I can feel my cheeks getting redder and redder and the panic welling up in my throat. Everyone is cheering around us and suddenly I have to break free from him. 'Just turn and walk away,' I keep telling myself. I don't think I ever lived that kiss down. 'You were kissing him like you were fighting for your life!' my friends said to me for *ages*.

The funny thing was, Ben had twin brothers called Ryan and Aaron and at some point down the line, I ended up kissing both of them along with their eldest brother who was seven years older than me. I joke that I was biding my time, and he didn't escape Marnie's clutches either!

Compared to other girls at secondary, though, I was quite innocent. A lot of them said they'd had sex with boys, but I reckon most of them were telling porkies. There was definitely pressure on girls to sleep with someone, and they used to call me frigid because I never had. I used to pretend I had, just to get them off my back, but I had no clue what I was talking about. I'd never even seen a boy's willy, let alone had it anywhere near me!

Strangely, I developed boobs quite early on and I was dead self-conscious about them, especially because I was still trampolining up until my early teens. My coach would always be nagging at me to buy a bra because they would jiggle up and down and I'd have to cup them with each hand before every jump. It was soooooo painful! No one else seemed to have boobs then, but if you turn to the pictures in this book, I bet you'll be surprised at what a chubby child I was – or at least I thought I was! There's one picture of me in a dress me nana bought me before her and Grandad took me back to Florida when I was thirteen. It's a gorgeous, pink-check dress with butterflies embroidered on it, and I adored it because I could twirl around in it. Now when I look at myself, all I see is a fat belly and boobs!

In truth, I didn't even start my period until I was almost fourteen, although lots of the girls at school had started at eleven – way before me.

When my period eventually did arrive, I was over the moon! I thought it was never going to come. Something must be horribly wrong with me, I kept thinking. All the girls had moaned about cramps and sore stomachs and whenever I felt an iota of pain I'd think, 'Yeesss! I am a woman!' That quickly turned to disappointment when I checked my knickers in the school toilets, and there was absolutely zilch there. When it did come, I went straight to tell me mam. She'd always been really open about 'women's things' and, anyway, she was paranoid I'd get pregnant young so she was always having 'the chat' with me about being careful if I ever had sex. What she didn't realise is how terrified I was about boys back then. I've certainly made up for it now, though!

Of the boys I did fancy, I had seriously bad taste. Even though there was *definitely no sex*, I did bring boys home, which Mam was fine with. They were never very nice boys, though. There was one called Ryan Ebanks and Mam hated him. She used to let him come over and hang out in my room, but she and I would be at each other's throats over him afterwards. 'He's no good for you, Marnie!' she'd say. But would I listen? No way! What do I think about him now? A complete waste of space, but there was no telling me that back then. He was three years older and he and his friends were into taking loads of drugs, which I wasn't. And I found out he was cheating on me, too. Despite knowing all of that, I was like this pathetic, love-sick puppy. He even had green teeth. Eeeewww! But I used to think he was so handsome. Sadly, I was so desperate for him to love me, I would put up with any shit from him. I used to phone him all the time, but when he began ignoring my calls, I knew he was seeing other girls. According to Mam she used to hear me in the bath, crying my eyes out over him and she was secretly keeping her fingers crossed that I'd dump him, but I was far too stubborn for that! Thankfully, it fizzled out in the end.

Then there was a lad called Kieran Temples, who I had a teenage fling with. He was very sweet and we did try to have sex in my bedroom. What a disaster that was! Picture the scene: squished onto my single bed with a badly sprung mattress surrounded by lilac wallpaper and a big heart-shaped rug. After a few awkward fumbles, both of us realised it wasn't going to happen. He was hard but I was scared rigid and every time he got close to getting his willy in, it was just too painful and uncomfortable. As a consolation, I ended up dry humping his leg like a terrier on heat. I remember thinking, 'What the hell am I doing?' I kept going, but what was the point to it? It was clumsy and awkward and I don't think either of us enjoyed it. The hilarious thing is that Kieran is out and proud now. He's even got a boyfriend. I wonder whether it was me that turned him!

I didn't actually lose my virginity until I was sixteen, which was really late compared to all my friends. Fortunately, it wasn't the wham-bam-thank-you-ma'am kind of sex some of them had reported. Instead, it was with a boy called Glenn who I was head over heels in love with.

Glenn is the boy I would class as my first serious relationship. We met in a nightclub when I was fifteen and he was eighteen. Even though I was underage, Sophie's friends would help me get into places, particularly one club in South Shields right on the seafront called Vogue where Glenn was a DJ. That was so cool! Back then, I used to wear more make-up than I do now but, even with loads of slap on, I'd have trouble getting in. With no proper ID of my own, Sophie used to get her hand stamped by the security guards, then go into the club for fifteen minutes, come back out and meet me in the kebab shop next door and pass me her ID. I swear it never failed!

Sometimes I'd go with my friend Rio who was my kind of crazy. She was a school friend of mine, but we never went to the same school. She was at St Wilfred's, which was the Roman Catholic secondary school across the road. We got chatting one day because we used to hang out together in Simply 2 Delicious, the sandwich shop on the corner where we'd have lunch. She was so happy-go-lucky and fun and a very loyal friend. We'd have these mad dreams about moving to America – to Miami or Los Angeles – and starring in *The Hills*, the reality TV programme we were glued to that followed girls in LA who wanted to make it in the fashion industry. Rio, along with my friend Lorna, were definitely the two friends I connected with the most.

Once I was inside Vogue, it felt like I was on top of the world. All the old club classics would be blaring out of the speakers and we'd dance our heads off. Beforehand, we'd spend hours getting ready. Not only did I have centimetre-thick foundation on my face, and so much cream blusher that I looked like a post-box, but there was one time when Rio and I put five pairs of lashes on. They were super-thick and so heavy we could hardly keep our eyes open. And we went out dressed in our lingerie! No joke. I wore a red lace bralette and a little frilly skirt with bright red stilettos. Of course, I thought I looked *a-mazing*. Basically, I was a child going out in her underwear!

All the girls fancied Glenn, and I'd only admired him from afar. I never thought in a million years he'd be interested in me. But one evening, in between his sets, he came over to chat to us. He started by taking the piss. 'Oh, Marnie and Rio, you must be dead exotic! What kind of names are those?' I'm sure that was just an excuse to talk to us. Rio had white blonde hair and she was so pretty I assumed he was after her. *All* the boys fancied Rio. When he asked me for my number, I was taken aback but I'd had a bit to drink so I was acting all blasé. He gave me his, too, and he started texting me the next day. Oh my God, he was soooooo handsome. Living in the North East, it's not like anyone has a tan seeing that it rains most of the time. But Glenn had the most lovely olive skin, sparkly blue eyes and thick dark hair, and he was dead tall. When he asked me if I wanted to go to the cinema, I was like, 'Will the sun rise tomorrow? Of course!' When he picked me up I didn't have half as much make-up on as I did the night he met me, and I could barely show him my face. 'What are you doing?'

he was laughing as I was covering my eyes. 'Don't be daft, you're absolutely gorgeous.' Awwwww! That was exactly what I wanted to hear.

The film we went to see was *Taken* – an all-action thriller starring Liam Neeson. Not that I remember much about the film at all. I had butterflies for the whole time and we kept brushing our hands and the sides of our legs together. That felt loads more romantic than any of the boys I'd ever been with. And he used to pick me up in his Ford Mondeo. A lad with wheels was definitely a step up from my usual, and I felt so cool when he'd get me from school.

If I'm honest, sex itself was quite confusing. Apart from the odd fumble and the unfortunate dry humping of Kieran Temples, I had literally no idea what I was doing. I remember lying back and not really moving, thinking I should just get it over and done with. It wasn't because I didn't fancy Glenn or anything; it was more I was far too uptight to enjoy it. It's not as if I knew how to let go and experiment. Like I said, I was a late bloomer and I've definitely come into my own in that department over the last few years!

Glenn was also a very steady guy, which is why Mam got on with him. He worked nine-to-five as an electrician and he was earning good money too, maybe as much as £400 a week, which at that age was a lot!

At sixteen, I left school without a single qualification. I didn't even turn up to my exams. I'm not saying I don't regret that now. I wish, wish, wish I'd tried harder at school. That way I would know a lot more and I would have had more opportunities, but I'm not a girl to have regrets. Anyway, I'd run a million miles from school, even now, I hated it so much. Unbelievably, I wasn't even allowed to go to my final year prom because I'd been on report constantly. That was disappointing because I was supposed to go with one of the boys from class and I'd spent ages dreaming of a dress. Now, when I think of all the black-tie dos and posh parties I've been to with *Geordie Shore*, I don't care that I didn't go to my prom, but at the time, being excluded felt like a *really* big deal.

The bottom line was that my relationship with Glenn was a nice, innocent one. It was normal, even though normal felt a bit odd to me. We were both totally into one another and he was one of those lads who encouraged me to be my best self. Despite failing everything at school, I was determined to make something of my life so I applied to go to South Tyneside College to study beauty therapy. I didn't think I'd have a hope in hell of getting in, but I went for an interview with tutor Karen Cummings, and I totally smashed it!

The minute I met her it was like she was completely on my level. Whereas in school, teachers would constantly be asking me to take my make-up off, she was telling me to put it on! My personality helped, I think. I remember talking non-stop and I was dead friendly and smiled loads because I knew it was my only chance. Whatever the reason, she didn't say 'no' to me and she wanted me to start that September. All through the summer, Glenn was brilliant at helping me with a routine. I was so healthy. I drank loads of water and went to the gym every day and we'd go out and have fun with our friends at the weekend. The whole of my six years at secondary school had been an uphill struggle, but for the first time ever I felt like I was finally in a good place.

That summer I also got my first tattoos. I wasn't squeamish about it at all, or afraid of the pain. I just kept thinking of the end result. For ages I'd been thinking I'd like to pay tribute to Mam. After all, she'd stuck with me through everything. So, on my upper back I had written, 'If you don't believe in angels, you haven't met my mother.' When she saw it, she was overwhelmed. On my inner arm, my second tattoo read, 'Never a failure, always a lesson.' I'd like to get that one removed now, but when I first got it done I loved the quote. Actually, it sums me up perfectly because if I spent my time regretting what I'd done or hadn't done, I'd never be where I am now.

College was the chance I'd been waiting for. As soon as I enrolled I loved it. At school, I got sent home every single day that I wore make-up but here it was the complete opposite. Every morning, I'd make sure my fake tan was even, my nails were done perfectly and my hair was styled. Typical me, I was so careful when walking the five minutes from home to college, so I didn't have a hair out of place when I arrived. And I had this lovely crisp, white uniform too, like a little pinny.

The most bizarre thing was that I turned up to every single class. If only my teachers could see me now, I kept thinking. Those two years of studying beauty therapy were the happiest time of my life. Lessons started at nine a.m. and finished at five p.m. with a half day on a Wednesday. Waxing, spray-tanning, eyebrow-shaping; you name it, we did it. In my first year, I got my NVQ1, which was the first qualification I'd ever got! I was buzzing!

And that year Dad started to become more involved in my life, too. Since moving to South Shields I'd not seen him or Nana and Grandad nearly as much as I had when we lived in Stanley. I still loved to visit, but every weekend was now spent with Glenn and my friends. Dad had also gone through a divorce from his wife and he'd suffered periods of unhappiness. I think he found it hard to come to terms with not seeing his sons, Ben and Daniel, as much. It's not like we'd ever been close, but Dad's always been a part of my life and when he offered to take Glenn and me to Benidorm for a long weekend, I was made up by the gesture. Dad wanted to reconnect and I knew he was trying hard to reach out. The bottom line was I'd missed out on so many years with him, I would have gone anywhere to make up for that.

The reality of Benidorm was slightly different, though. The hotel and the pool were lovely, and for the first few nights it was dead exciting going out drinking on The Strip. Even if I came home early, Glenn and Dad would go to the next bar and hang out together. Relationships weren't, and still aren't, something I'd ever talk to Dad about, but I was pleased I was with Glenn on our first holiday together and chuffed that he and Dad got along.

Everything was going brilliantly until the last night when I left Glenn and Dad out drinking together and me dad vanished. Typically, parents should be sat in worrying about their kids, but not Dad. That's not his style at all. Instead, Glenn came home saying he'd left him with a party of Spanish women. He was shouting to Glenn, 'Don't worry about me. I'll be home later.' But we were flying out early the next day and I had this sinking feeling. Shit! Will he come home?

Sure enough, Dad didn't reappear for the rest of the night. When I checked his room the next morning, he still hadn't turned up, and he wasn't picking up his phone either. We frantically stuffed all his clothes into his suitcase, but in my heart, I didn't expect to see him. 'We're going to have to leave without him,' I told Glenn sadly as we booked a taxi to the airport.

Leaving Dad in Benidorm was the last thing we wanted to do, but we had no choice. Funnily, I didn't feel let down by him; it was more that I wanted him with us. It was so sweet that he'd offered to take us on holiday and although Dad wasn't very good at showing love, I'd got used to him being kind in his own way.

Just as we were about to haul the suitcases to the hotel lobby, he strolled in like there was nowt to bother. He was so chilled he was almost horizontal.

'Dad!' I shouted.

'What?' he replied, looking a bit baffled.

'I've been calling you non-stop!'

'It's not like I was ever going to miss the flight!' he had the cheek to say.

I never did find out exactly what he'd been doing, but by the look of him, he'd been up all night dancing in the mountains. I think it's really funny now. Like father, like daughter!

Although mine and Glenn's relationship was brilliant, it was tested very early on. South Shields' nightlife was often about going to house parties, given that Vogue and a club called the Biz Bar were the only places to get mortal. But there was one house party that ended in tragedy, and although Glenn and I weren't there, I don't think he or the community ever got over it. Whereas I hadn't ever dabbled with drugs then, for other friends, taking cocaine and pills and MD was a normal weekend. That night loads of our friends had been out to a cage-fighting show at the arena in nearby Houghton-le-Spring and piled back to Glenn's friend Callum Taylor's flat, which was in quite a rough part of South Shields. Not long after, Callum collapsed on the floor and his other friend, a lad called Ryan Burn, was found unconscious in his flat round the corner. Callum was dead within hours of the ambulance being called and Ryan lost his life a week later, both of suspected organ failure. Callum was only twenty-four and Ryan was twenty and after the inquest it emerged that they'd died from taking a cocktail of drugs including Ecstasy, MDMA, and the amphetamine BZP.

When Glenn took the call, he was absolutely devastated and it scared a lot of people locally, too – especially people our age. Drugs were all around. If we wanted them, we knew where to get them, but friends dying was a whole new ball game that no one was prepared for. Everybody swears it will never happen to them, but Callum and Ryan are the proof that it can.

Both funerals were totally heart-wrenching. Hundreds of mourners turned up to support the families and Glenn helped carry Ryan's coffin into the crematorium. He wasn't the same for a long time afterwards, and I reckon those deaths probably still affect him now. It was like this black cloud hanging over South Shields, and especially awful for Ryan's family as his dad had been murdered in a gangland killing three years before.

I remember standing watching the horse-drawn carriage carrying Ryan's body and all I kept thinking was that those deaths could have been avoided. When you're young and out partying you never think of the dangers, but after that, I never thought about taking drugs the same way again.

CHAPTER 5

MAM'S GONE

For all the time I was with Glenn, and for as long as I could remember, Mam was on her own. It used to really hurt me. Rio would be around, and we'd be getting changed and putting our slap on in front of the bathroom mirror, and Mam would be watching soaps in the room next door. 'Bye, Mam. See you later,' I'd shout as we closed the door behind us. My heart always sank when I'd hear her call back, 'Bye, pet. Have a good night.' She never came out with us and I always used to think, 'Why can't Mam meet someone? Why can't she be happy?' All those years of looking after me and not having any money or a steady job had really affected her self-confidence. And once we moved to South Shields, she didn't have a lot of friends either.

Like any typical seventeen-year-old, I was caught up in my own dramas. I loved Glenn and he treated me really well, always buying me gifts and being there emotionally. OK, spoiler alert. If I'm going to tell my story, then I'm going to have to man up and admit my mistakes too.

The truth is, I got bored. I was going out more, having fun and that was that. One night, the love goggles were on and – *bam!* – I met a guy who was soooooo good-looking. One minute he'd rocked up, and the next I'd persuaded all my mates to stay at the bar for the night. Unbeknown to them, I had my eyes on the prize – him! And I didn't leave empty-handed. I'd not slept with anyone on a first night before. In fact, I was quite terrified about it, but this lad was not only insanely gorgeous, he was flirtatious and dead exciting too. If there's one saying that I would use here, it's the one about being a moth to a flame. Before I knew it, we were hailing down a cab and heading to a hotel of all places. While we were necking on in the back seat, my phone was vibrating in my bag, flashing with missed calls from Glenn. Poor, poor guy had been trying to get in touch with me the whole night, but I ignored the calls. As I say, not my finest moment.

Anyway, on the morning after I woke up in the hotel, I picked up my mobile and saw a text from Glenn asking where I was and announcing he was coming over to talk things through. Talk things through? Fuck! Only Mam was at home! I was so hungover, but I leaped out of bed, yanked on my bra, knickers and dress, and legged it home. Sneakily, I came in through Mam's back door and went up the stairs, throwing my clothes on my bed as I ran. Only moments before the doorbell sounded, I'd shoved on my pyjamas and jumped into bed and under the covers with Mam.

'Glenn's going to come over, and I've spent all night with another lad,' I hurriedly confessed, making sure she was up to speed before the fireworks began.

'You really are a little shit, Marnie,' she said, rolling her eyes, because Mam liked Glenn and she didn't want to see him hurt.

Reluctantly, I let Glenn in and I brought him up to my room. Mam moved to the living room, battening down the hatches against the drama about to unfold next door. Bizarrely, there weren't any fireworks, which was almost worse! I didn't need to say anything. I think he could tell from my eyes that something had happened and we were over.

'I'm sorry,' I mumbled, and with that he legged it downstairs, slamming the front door behind him. We've never talked again, which I feel sad about now.

'Poor lad didn't deserve that, Marnie,' I could hear Mam saying disapprovingly from the sofa. There's nothing like your mam to make you feel as guilty as hell!

She was right, but the moral of the story is I got what I deserved in the end. Someone somewhere wanted to punish me. I totally believe in karma because the next couple of years were awful.

Before I get into that, though, I want to tell you about Mam; because while I was about to embark on probably the craziest relationship of my life, she was about to meet the love of hers.

Unbeknown to me, she'd been internet dating and got talking to a man who lived in Las Vegas. When she spilled the beans, I was just pleased she'd been talking to someone or had even been thinking about dating men because it was my dream that she'd meet someone amazing! But Las Vegas? That was on the other side of the world! I didn't reckon this relationship would go anywhere, but I was never going to say that. She was already nervous about telling me.

Mam seemed dead keen on this guy called Eric and they'd even started messaging each other. Turned out he was a couple of years younger and when she showed me his profile picture, he looked handsome and kind. I was secretly keeping my fingers crossed, but I didn't want to build the Eric thing up too much because I was terrified Mam would be so let down if the contact suddenly stopped.

Meanwhile, I started seeing this guy called Mark. My relationship with him was like a whirlwind. He was really good looking, had this ginger hair and the most amazing blue eyes. He was really tall and skinny, not at all like the kind of guy I'd go for. Plus he owned his own car, which made him seem really grown up. It's every girl's dream to feel swept off their feet, and I was; but a few months into our relationship I was starting to notice another side to him. Don't get me wrong, Mark had this lovely front and he was very charismatic and generous – always offering drinks to me and my friends if we were out. He was not exactly a party animal, which is why I was surprised I couldn't resist him. But he was one thing from early on, and that's possessive.

I'd made friends with some of the girls on my course and I was still seeing Sophie and all her friends, but he hated me going out with them and he'd always try to stop me. There was this jealous streak. For example, he paid for everything because it's not like I had much cash being unemployed. If we went out for something to eat, he always offered to foot the bill, but the way I see it now is that him paying for everything seemed like a power trip to him, some sort of emotional blackmail.

This one time, I remember being in a restaurant with him and he said he'd only eat with me if I agreed to sit facing the wall.

'What?' I asked, completely gobsmacked.

'Face the wall because I don't want you looking at anyone else,' he said.

God knows why, but at the time, I agreed. *What the fuck?* I was starting to feel scared by him. When I think about it now, his behaviour was seriously disturbing. There's no way I'd put up with that now! What was most telling was I didn't talk to Mam about him, and I talked to Mam about *everything*. Part of the problem was I didn't want to bring her down. She was having her own romance, even if it was online, and her and Eric were now FaceTiming each other every night. I was over the moon for her and I didn't want to burden her with my shit. Also, because Mam's really protective of me and she's a total hothead, I kept putting off having that conversation.

At the beginning of summer, Sophie said she wanted a girls' holiday and was planning on flying out to Ayia Napa. Naturally, I wanted to go. Girls, The Strip, vodka and partying was exactly what I needed. As it was early days with Mark, I didn't expect him to have a problem with it. He didn't, but I sensed he wasn't comfortable with the idea. Despite his weird demands, we'd never argued and we were still in the honeymoon phase and quite shy around each other, so perhaps he was holding back.

Ayia Napa was a ball! It was my first real girls' holiday and I totally let go. 'Messy' is the only way I can describe The Strip – packed with bars and nightclubs and masses of stag parties, and lads and lasses getting mortal and spewing on pavements. Some of those pavements were decorated by yours truly! One night we ended up dancing in a club, but I was palatic and started necking on with a lad who was working out there as a PR. I don't even remember his name, but he was dead friendly and it was sultry hot and we just got carried away. It's not like we slept with each other or anything, so I planned not to tell Mark about it. It was nothing but a drunken kiss.

On the day I was due to come home, Mark texted me to ask what time my flight was due in to Newcastle as he wanted to pick me up. After a week of abusing my body with booze, I was glad to be home, and I was genuinely pleased to see him.

As I came through customs, I could see him waiting to welcome me. I rushed to hug him, but as we were walking towards the car he started asking me all these questions. He wouldn't shut up. If I'm honest, it was starting to weird me out a bit.

'Did you have a good time, babe?' he asked.

'Yeah, it was great. Missed you, though,' I replied.

'Did you neck on with anyone?' he carried on.

'No,' I said at first, but he was full-on questioning me.

'If you did kiss someone, I won't be angry. We can move on. If it's one mistake, I won't care.'

In the end, he wore me down, and I did feel guilty about the guy in the club.

'Yes, but it was just a kiss,' I eventually confessed.

By that time he was driving and for a moment there was silence in the car. Suddenly his hand came from nowhere towards my head and he belted me across the face. I almost dropped the coke I was holding. My body tensed up. I was in utter shock. 'Take me home,' I ordered him. As soon as his car pulled up, I got out, slammed the door shut, hauled my suitcase off the back seat and walked towards my front door without turning around to look at him. I know he hated that; he was that insecure.

Apparently, I found out later one of the girls I was in Ayia Napa with had told her friend I'd kissed someone at a beach party and they had told Mark. All that time, he'd been waiting for me to confess. In his head, I think it gave him some sort of licence to batter me.

I knew I'd behaved badly, but I didn't deserve that. No excuses. Hitting anyone is plain wrong. My advice to any other girls faced with an abusive boyfriend? Leave him. If it's verbal abuse or a kick or a punch or a slap, you should walk away because as soon as a person has done that once, they'll do it again. Unless they get help, I don't think it stops. But I also understand how easy it is to say that, and how hard it is to do it. Looking back, my relationship with Mark was the start of a lot of my own insecurities. He made me feel worthless.

After Ayia Napa, Mark hated me going out with my mates even more. He didn't even want me to spend time with me mam! The daft thing was, I went along with it. Now Mam says it was really hard for her to stand by and watch. Even though we'd not really spoken about it, she knew how awful he made me feel, and she often witnessed our blazing rows. We were like two lost people tearing strips off each other.

Then Sophie announced she wanted to spend a whole season working in Ayia Napa because she'd had such a good time on our girls' holiday. After the way Mark had behaved, the headstrong part of me thought, why the hell not? Perhaps subconsciously I also wanted to put some distance between us. But I was terrified of how he might react. I walked on eggshells for days plucking up the courage to tell him. Surprisingly, he accepted it. But could he still ruin that summer without even being there?

For days after arriving in Ayia Napa, I was constantly on edge. I had this eerie fear that Mark was going to turn up out of the blue. Sophie and the other two girls we travelled with, Chrissy and Claire, didn't help my nerves either. They knew how possessive he was, and they were always telling me to get rid. As a joke, every so often one of them would look out of our apartment window and shout: 'Look! Look! Mark's outside!'

'Where? Where?' I'd jump out of my skin, before I realised they were winding me up. In the end it became a running gag, but I was so anxious I'd fall for it every time.

Despite my fears, Ayia Napa was the pick-me-up I needed. The brilliant thing about The Strip there is that it's so lively and, other than the heat, you wouldn't even know you were abroad. It's packed full of English people all out to have a good time. I've never seen so many men! Honestly, the ratio of lads to lasses is around three to one. Compared to Ibiza and Marbella, it's probably a bit sleazy, but you can have a right laugh there. Whether I'd enjoy it now, I don't know, but back then it was definitely the place to be. Pitching up with a suitcase to find work for the season was so simple, and the minute we landed, Sophie, Chrissy and Claire bagged this two-bedroomed apartment right on The Strip. Not that I ever wanted to work! Once we were there, the temptation to sloth and sunbathe all day and party all night was huge.

Er . . . reality check, Marnie. We needed to eat! After an hour or so trailing around the bars and restaurants asking for work, I got a job in a bar called

Crystals which was the very first bar you arrived at on The Strip. Although it was mega busy, I found it boring. Also, Chrissy had got a job in a place called Mambos which was a few metres further down and she was having much more fun. After a couple of weeks, I jacked in my job at Crystals and joined her there. Mambos was a lot bigger and it even had one of those rodeo bulls in the bar so if we were really bored we'd pretend to be cowgirls and get astride the bucking bronco.

Despite the bar being better, I still hated working and I realised I was not the sort of person to enjoy working a season. Most of the clientele in the bars were palatic lads on stag parties who we'd serve shots to or podium dance for. Once I was on shift, I'd have a few drinks, but I couldn't get drunk. I wanted to have the best time without any of the pain! Forget work, I kept thinking, I want to go bar-hopping! The amount of times I rang me nana to ask her to send money was ridiculous. And she would always send it, but I did take the piss! One time, we were so broke that the four of us did topless dancing for one night for the money – but we got ripped off.

A guy walked into Mambos and came straight out with it. 'Do you girls want to earn four hundred euros a night stripping?'

'Yeah! We just have to dance and take our tops off?'

We were so naive. And it was the most degrading

thing I've ever done. This guy's bar was so sleazy and we had to pole dance, even though we were all shit. Sophie got it the worst. All the old, bald men gravitated towards her and we spent the whole night laughing and taking the piss. Did we ever get paid? Nah. He must have seen us coming!

I even met this lad called Matty who I had a bit of a summer romance with. We didn't sleep together. We just kissed and hung out with each other. He was friendly and it was casual, and had it not been for Mark always in the shadows texting me, maybe I would have shagged him, but sadly I was too paranoid. What Ayia Napa did show me, though, was I could have a life without Mark. In the end, when I'd completely run out of money and I was forced to go home, I promised myself I wouldn't go back to him. Which, of course, I stuck to for about two minutes! As soon as we saw each other again, we were back to the same sad routine that I couldn't break free from.

One of the nice bits about going home was seeing me mam. While I'd been away, she and Eric had been getting really close. I even heard them saying, 'Love you' whenever they FaceTimed in the evening. There was never a moment when I felt jealous of Eric or I wanted Mam to myself. I was completely made up for her, but it did mean the only other person I had close in my life was Mark, and we ended up spending all our time together.

When Eric eventually did come over to visit Mam, I liked him immediately. Not only was he very tall and handsome, but he was the polar opposite to Mam: calm, easy-going and an insanely positive person. The weird thing was he had this deep American accent, like John Wayne off the old cowboy films, and he made Mam and me feel so protected. I loved me dad, but I guess he was never around for me in the same way. Eric felt like part of our family from the off. I always say I'm lucky I've got two dads.

Not long after Eric came to stay with Mam, she broke it to me that she wanted to fly over and give the relationship a go in Las Vegas. I was eighteen, I had my own life, so I understood her decision. I was surprised, though. Her relationship with Eric had happened quickly and now everything that had seemed impossible to start with had become possible. When she told me, I wasn't upset. I didn't even cry. I just said, 'That's OK, Mam. I'm pleased for you.' Now, when I think about it, I'd blocked all the emotion out. According to her, she was gutted by my reaction. Because I acted so blasé, she assumed I didn't care. At the time, I was so wrapped up in Mark and under his toxic spell that I wasn't thinking straight.

Within weeks, Mam had a flight booked from Newcastle and we took her to the bus station to see her off. Everything Mam owned was packed into one suitcase. I kissed her, and we promised to ring each other every day. There was part of me, though, that wanted to tell her there and then about Mark and about how unhappy I was, but I knew if I did, she'd cancel her flight on the spot and I'd ruin her new life with the man she loved. Instead, I pretended it wasn't happening and Mam wasn't leaving. I hated Mark that day, smiling and hugging her and telling her he was going to take care of me and she wasn't to worry. The minute the bus edged out of the station and Mam was out of sight, I knew he'd turn back to the jealous, controlling boyfriend he was before.

With Mam gone, I needed money and so I took work with Ash Care & Nursing, which was an agency that hired help for old people's homes. It couldn't have been more different from my placements in beauty salons. Every week I was given my rota, which involved some days spent in the home and others looking after elderly people in their homes. That job really affected me. Each time I walked through the door, I saw all these people alone. Some of them were hardly able to move. Others hadn't a clue where they were or they had Alzheimer's and didn't know their own names. Plus, it's not even funny how obsessed I was with getting old and dying alone, so being surrounded by it all got under my skin.

I remember one man had severe OCD and if I didn't fold the corners of his bed correctly, he'd get so angry he'd make the bed shake. He couldn't speak so he'd just clench his fists and rattle the frame. Because he was so scary we always tried to work in pairs when we tended to him.

Another woman I used to go and visit in a block of flats in South Shields had Parkinson's disease, and a whole list of other medical conditions too. She was unable to do anything for herself, so there would be two of us massaging her legs and helping her to the toilet and feeding her. Her daughter-in-law was beautiful, but I used to hear her crying in her room a lot. She was foreign and she'd come to England with no friends and two children and now she was living in this God-awful place with her mother-in-law who was desperately ill. After seeing her, I'd have a major depression session. My shifts were long and hard and I always left the job feeling emotionally drained.

More and more, my life outside work was with Mark, and I'd even started to cut off my friends. I was in this vicious cycle of arguing with him and then making up. But the arguments were becoming worse and more violent. We decided to move in together which was the stupidest thing I could have agreed to because now that flat felt like a prison.

One night, on one of the rare times I did go out with my friends, I borrowed a lad's jacket to keep me warm while we waited for a taxi, only I'd accidentally come home still wearing it. Sophie was there with a crowd of mates, and this lad was just being kind. Mark was waiting up for me, and as soon as I got home and he saw the jacket, he flipped.

'What the fuck are you wearing?' he asked.

'Oh, a lad loaned it to me. I forgot to give it back,' I said innocently.

Immediately, he marched past me and locked the front door. Suddenly, I felt his hand grasp my hair. He yanked it so hard, it pulled me to the ground and although I kicked and screamed, he refused to let go. That night he dragged me by my hair from room to room. It was absolutely terrifying. He'd turned into a monster, punching and kicking me and calling me evil names. I had no idea how far he would go.

'Please stop,' I kept screaming, but it took hours for him to calm down. He kept saying insane things like he'd drive his car off a cliff with us both in it, and I was so scared that I believed him.

Despite the beatings he gave me, I'd convinced myself that I loved Mark and I needed to be with him. Crazy, huh? I'd always justify it by telling myself he looked after me. Anything I wanted, he bought me.

After one argument, he even bought me a car! He knew I'd always wanted one and he'd paid £2,000 for it. Normally I would have loved that present, but my stomach turned over the minute I saw it and I couldn't bear to get in it. Thinking about it now, that tells me a lot about how unhappy I was in the relationship.

After a couple of weeks, I hadn't used the car once and I said to Mark he should sell it because I'd never want to drive it.

After that, our arguments got worse and worse, and Mark was becoming more unpredictable. He'd frequently smash the place up and hold me by the throat against the wall. I never took his abuse lying down and I always tried to defend myself, but the bottom line was, he was far, far stronger than me.

By now, the neighbours had had enough, and they would frequently call the police when the screaming and crashing became too much. Typically, I would pretend like nothing was happening and we were just having a tiff, but underneath I was so embarrassed. Soon I started getting letters off the housing association saying there had been complaints about the noise and if things didn't improve, we'd be kicked out for good.

Although Mam and I were always talking over the phone, I never told her anything. I missed her so much, but the last thing I wanted was for her to come home. When the final warning dropped through the letter box, I was devastated. I had nowhere to go, no money and I was clinging on to Mark because I'd convinced myself that he was the only person left in my life.

CHAPTER 6

VIVA LAS VEGAS!

The last place I ever thought I'd end up again was Stanley, but that's exactly what happened. I quit my job with the agency, lost Mam's flat and moved back in with me nana and grandad. No job. No money. No car. And to top it all, I was back in the place that I'd spent years dreaming of escaping. Most of my friends had moved from Stanley, so it's not like I had anyone my age around me. Sadly, moving home didn't mean Mark was out of my life, either. We couldn't seem to separate ourselves from each other and he'd often drive down and stay over.

Of course, Nana and Grandad were quite conservative and he never argued with me in front of them or ever raised a hand to me. For that reason, I'm sure I clung on to him for far longer than I should have done. I could hear myself making excuses for him in my head, like he didn't mean the things he said or did, and even blaming myself for his abuse. That's how bad a state my head was in! The constant cycle of arguing then making up wore me down over time. Why is it that the worst men get under your skin and you can't easily say goodbye to them?

All the time I'd been refusing to think about Mam leaving, but now it hit me hard. Every time I missed her, I'd stop myself dwelling on it and call Mark instead. When she and I did speak, she told me how worried she was about me, that I didn't sound normal and I seemed moody. I'm sure Nana had been talking to her too. Although I didn't recognise it at the time, I was so depressed. And I'd started losing loads of weight.

When I was growing up, Nana and Grandad's was the place where I looked forward to being well fed. They were such amazing cooks, and other than being a chubby teenager until the age of thirteen when all my puppy fat disappeared, I was a healthy size ten. Now, I was getting close to an unhealthy size six. My arms looked like coat hangers. Although I never went as far as making myself sick, I became so obsessed with my weight that if I even had so much as a chip, it would play on my mind for ages and I'd have to go to the gym. The only way I can describe it was like being in a trance. I needed to snap out of it but I didn't know how.

By now, Nana and Grandad were really worried about me too, although I still never told them the truth. They must have thought I hated living back at theirs, but my depression wasn't because of them. Having said that, they insisted on me giving them £20 a week for my board. Because I was on the dole, that meant I had no freedom to do anything and it made me rely on Mark even more. I understand now that they wanted me to stand on my own two feet, but I remember getting so angry with me grandad, shouting at him and saying, 'Why do you keep taking money off us?'

After a few months, I couldn't hide my moods any longer, and crying myself to sleep in the privacy of my room turned into crying down the phone to Mam. 'I'm coming home,' Mam said. But I pleaded with her to stay with Eric. Unbeknown to me, she was driving herself demented with guilt and making plans to get a flight back to England. The whole situation nearly broke her and Eric up because she was so upset about the state I'd got myself into. Now I know how close she was to giving up her relationship, I have even more love for her. And it's made me appreciate how tough it is being a parent – especially a parent to me!

Then, one evening she said she and Eric had been talking and they wanted me to come to Las Vegas.

I could come for a couple of months to see if I liked it and, if I did, I could stay. At first I jumped at the idea but, as I say, I was in such a weird place that the offer of a lifetime turned out to be wasted.

What was good, however, was that I was away from Mark, and I felt dead proud of myself that I'd managed the long-haul flight on my own. Mam and Eric were there waiting for me at the other end, and I'll never forget Mam's face when I walked through the exit in Las Vegas. She couldn't hide her shock at how painfully thin I was.

Other than totally fucking up school, if there's one thing that I wish I could turn the clock back and make better, it is my Las Vegas trip. Ever since I was a little girl and Nana and Grandad took me to Florida, I'd loved America, and now I had this amazing opportunity of staying. Did I give a shit? No! Mam's love for me is unreal, but on that trip, I really didn't deserve it.

As much as she and Eric were so nice to me, it was like a different person had landed on their doorstep. I wasn't interested in them, or going out with them. I'd transformed into this dark, bitter and angry teenager. I was also still obsessed with Mark and I'd FaceTime him at every opportunity telling him how much I wanted to be back home with him.

Occasionally, I'd go to the drive-in movies with Mam and Eric, which I did love, and one night I even went out with Heather, the daughter of a guy Eric went ten-pin bowling with. They thought maybe being with someone of a similar age might do me good.

The legal drinking age is twenty-one in the States and I was too young to get into a club, but Heather loaned me some ID and took me out. She was dead bubbly and she introduced me to a place called The Chateau. Oh my God! I'd never been anywhere like it! It was a million miles away from Vogue or the Biz Bar in South Shields. I felt really nervous going past security, but we were all dressed up and I looked way older than nineteen. Thank fuck for make-up and heels! I shit you not, this club is in a replica of the Eiffel Tower with this huge roof garden where you can look out across the whole of Las Vegas and watch the neon lights of The Strip. Then we danced on the biggest dance floor I'd ever seen. Everyone looked amazing and glamorous and I felt a bit intimidated and not half as confident as everyone seemed around me. Halfway through the evening I thought Heather was going to explode!

'Look! Look! There's The Situation!' she kept shouting, but I had no idea what she was talking about.

'Who?' I was screaming over the music.

'It's The Situation from *Jersey Shore*!' she kept repeating, and by now she was totally buzzing.

It turned out that the guy she kept pointing to was from a US TV series called *Jersey Shore*, which everyone her age watched and which aired on MTV. The series followed eight housemates during the summer in New Jersey and this guy's real name was Mike Sorrentino. I've still no idea why his nickname is 'The Situation', but he was utterly gorgeous, dressed all in black with the coolest aviator glasses on. Apparently, he'd become one of the highest paid reality TV stars in the US since the show had started in 2009. What was more amazing was that he was doing a public appearance and DJing at the club *we* were dancing in. What were the chances of that? When I scanned the club, it was like everyone knew who he was and he was lapping up all the attention. Given the way Heather was going on, it might as well have been Justin Bieber who'd rocked up.

After he finished DJing, he was escorted into this cordoned off section of the club reserved for VIPs. God knows how I did it, but I only managed to blag us in! 'Can you let us in for a drink?' I shouted to security. I was so determined, my stilettos were already over the rope. I was going in whether they liked it or not! My lack of nerves was purely because I had no idea how much of a celebrity this guy was. Heather was made up. Now we weren't just looking at The Situation from afar, we were actually drinking with him and his entourage. We were buzzing! And we ended up going to his hotel suite for an after-party. Heather and I had to leg it from there, though, because we both kissed his mate – 'The Unit' – and he'd thought we were on for a threesome! A kiss is a kiss, but a threesome? No way. Besides, no one there seemed to have proper names!

The whole night felt so surreal, but what was even more weird was that Sophie rang me a couple of days later with some news.

'Marnie, you're not going to believe it. I've auditioned to be on TV,' she said sounding like she was about to burst.

'What the hell for?'

She explained to me that she'd seen this advert pop up on her Facebook page for a show called *Geordie Shore*. I don't remember the exact words but it was something like: '*Are you over eighteen and want to get drunk with a load of friends and party ALL summer?*' Well, that's a complete no-brainer! She hadn't had the audition yet, just an initial phone call, but she was over the moon.

'You're not going to believe it, Sophie, but I was in a club with the guy off *Jersey Shore* the other night,' I told her.

'*Geordie Shore*'s the English version of that!'

Sophie was dead excited, although it felt a bit like I'd stolen her thunder. I'd be the first to admit I was always jealous of Sophie's life. Her dad, Kevin, owned this lovely Italian restaurant in South Shields called Mambos and she always had money and new outfits and, by comparison, my life felt like a car crash. Nevertheless, I loved Sophie and I was pleased for her that she was doing something amazing rather than settling for helping her dad out serving drinks and waiting tables.

Talking about car crashes, Mark and I had been in touch and he said he was desperate for me to come home. I can't believe I fell for it, but he promised me things had changed and he'd found us a great place to rent in Gateshead so that I could leave Stanley and be with him again.

When I broke it to Mam that I was leaving Las Vegas two weeks earlier than planned, she was heartbroken. I couldn't have been in my right mind; I know how much she wanted me to stay, and that her and Eric had high hopes I would love it.

For the duration of the flight home I wasn't even missing Mam. All I kept thinking about was how Mark was a changed person and I didn't have to go back to Stanley. What an idiot! Life was about to get so much worse.

Instead of the cosy two-bedroomed house Mark had said he'd found for us, he picked me up from the airport and took me to one of the dingiest places I'd ever seen. It was ten times more depressing than anywhere me and Mam had ever lived. No joke, it was literally an abandoned flat above a dry-cleaners.

Above: Mam and Dad before I came along –
dead good-looking, aren't they?

A little bundle of cuteness – Me, aged 1.

Below: Mam, Nana and me in the middle.
No idea what's so interesting off camera –
always had the attention span of a goldfish.

Mam holding me in her arms, wearing her signature hoop earrings – I always think she looks gorgeous!

Below: Mam trying to steal my ice cream. I look fuming! Some things never change!

Christmas outfits – Mam and me.

Below: Posing in the garden with Mam on a rare sunny day in Stanley.

Although me dad wasn't around much, I know his heart was there.

Above: Some of the best bits of my childhood were just spending time with my family.

Nana and Grandad Simpson – they were always there for me growing up and I'm so grateful to them.

On my first ever trip abroad to Florida with Nana and Grandad Simpson.

Out for a "hack" with
the South Causey
Equestrian Centre – I
loved riding so much!

Trampolining was my
life growing up – I
even won medals!

We didn't have much, but Mam always tried her best!

Oh God! School photographs... I was so awkward.

Those teenage years – although I've never been a girly girl my bedroom was wall-to-wall pink!

Out on the town with Mam, Me, my cousin Sophie (haven't we changed?!) and Aunty Eunice.

When he turned the key in the lock and opened the door, I could smell the damp. My jaw dropped. It had no heating, no beds and no furniture whatsoever and he'd bought two sleeping bags for our bedroom so we could camp out on the floor.

'You've brought me here?' I said, confused.

'Yeah, babe. I told you I found us a place.'

'But you made out it was a proper house!'

'It'll do until we get on our feet.'

I felt gutted. I never asked or knew where he got it from, but Mark always had money to spend so I couldn't understand why he was putting me through this and why he'd lied to me. That first night, I remember lying beside him on the hard floor and thinking what I'd left behind: bright sunshine, wide roads, shopping malls, neon lights and the warmest atmosphere around Mam and Eric – even though I'd been a little devil child the whole time I'd been in Las Vegas. And now I was home to this – a horrible flat and a boyfriend who clearly didn't give a shit about me! I think I even lied to Mam when she rang me, saying Mark had got us this amazing place. From that moment on, I knew I had to leave him, but I was still stuck to him like a limpet. He was company. He was there for me. He paid for everything and I didn't want to be on my own. And I needed all those things so badly, I was willing to put up with his abuse. If I could go back in time, I'd give myself a good old slap!

Meanwhile, Sophie was so excited about her upcoming audition. The minute I was back, she asked if I would accompany her to Newcastle for the day for moral support. I said yes, but there was a part of me that didn't want to be faced with Sophie if she got it. For the whole journey to the Thistle Hotel I kept punishing myself in my head, asking why I hadn't seen the advert and why hadn't I applied? Don't get me wrong, I was really happy for Sophie but I suppose I was also desperate for my life to turn around.

At the audition, we had to wait for ages with loads of other hopefuls before Sophie's name was called. She was dead nervous and, at first, she'd wanted me to come into the room with the producers while they asked her questions. However, there was a strict 'no friends' policy so I waited around in the lobby. 'Go in there and smash it,' I encouraged her before giving her a big hug. Sophie was in there for ages, or at least it felt like ages, and I was on tenterhooks imagining all the questions she was being asked. I kept my eyes on the double doors waiting for when she emerged.

Beforehand, the crew had told her that auditionees wouldn't find out if they'd been successful on the day, but I reckoned they might give her the nod if she was in with a chance. When I saw her face beaming from ear to ear, I knew she'd done well. Apparently, the producers had told her she'd been brilliant, that she was a natural in front of the camera and they'd call her in the next few days.

Arrrggghhh! Sophie was so over the moon, she screamed all the way home with happiness! And the minute the confirmation email landed in her inbox she rang me. 'Oh my God! Oh my God!' she kept shouting.

Before any filming started she had to have a final interview with all the top people from London who were coming up to Newcastle. Sophie is so confident and drop dead gorgeous, though, I knew she'd sail through it. Sophie's life was about to take off, but mine wasn't going anywhere. Not only was I in the shitty flat with Mark, I still had no job. We'd even stopped having sex. If anyone asked me, I always said I loved him, but I couldn't bear it if he touched me or wanted to sleep with me.

In the end, I bit the bullet. I asked me Auntie Julie if I could have a room at hers, which she agreed to. I hadn't by this point seen Mark in a while but I couldn't close the door on Mark completely. We were still texting and, for the first time in ages, I knew this was the beginning of the end. Whereas before if Mark called me, I'd be desperate to answer, now my heart sank and talking to him felt like a chore. Phew! In some ways, Sophie starting filming on *Geordie Shore* was a good thing because as much as she was having a ball – meeting all these new people, and out partying – I thought if she could make something of herself, then so could I. The problem was, I hadn't worked out how yet!

Filming on *Geordie Shore* sounded mad! Sophie was locked in a house with seven others in this posh part of Newcastle called Jesmond – the area where all the footballers live.

While she was filming, she wasn't allowed a mobile phone, so we couldn't speak, but one night when I'd gone clubbing in Newcastle to a place called Bijoux, *Geordie Shore* was being filmed there! Seeing Sophie was amazing. Her hair and make-up looked so professional and there were runners everywhere fetching drinks and bringing them back to a cordoned-off VIP area. At first I didn't know whether Sophie would invite me in, but I was worrying over nothing. The first people she introduced me to were Charlotte Crosby and Vicky Pattison. Of course, back then I had no idea I was going to live with them in the *Geordie Shore* house. Eventually, when I did join the series and I was on their turf, they acted very differently, but that night everyone was so friendly. I particularly remember Charlotte being bubbly and loads of fun. She talked non-stop, whereas I found Vicky aloof and a bit intimidating – it's funny how gut feelings are often right! 'Hi. You're Sophie's baby cousin?' she asked as she looked me up and down and turned to talk to someone else. The funny thing was, I really wanted them to like me, even though I wasn't on the programme. I guess they all had this celebrity aura around them!

At times, I was on the sidelines watching all the action unfold as the cameraman moved around the crowd. And I was really taken aback by how Sophie and all her new mates could chat shit and be drunk and look totally cool on camera. It was almost as if they'd forgotten they were being filmed. How can they do that? I kept wondering. At one point the camera even panned on me, and I immediately wanted the ground to swallow me up. Hard to believe now, I know, but I was that shy!

That night I went home and made a resolution: I was going to sort myself out. Mark was almost out of my life, but I still had no job, no money and nothing to look forward to. Sophie, on the other hand, seemed to have the world at her feet.

Someone somewhere must have heard my prayers, because the next day I had a phone call from my friend Lowis offering me a job. Honestly, that girl is my guardian angel! And it was so like Lowis, too. Out of all my friends, she's the sensible one. I met her through Sophie when I was around fifteen, but it wasn't until a bit later that we got really close. Perhaps it's because Lowis is a year older than me, but she is always looking out for me. She knew I was in a bad way, and as she had also trained as a beautician she wanted me to work with her in Sunderland in a new salon she'd agreed to manage. Lowis drove a Ford Fiesta so she could pick me up every morning from me Auntie Julie's and drop me off. OK, it wasn't the bright lights of the *Geordie Shore* house, but I was back in South Shields and now I had a weekly pay cheque coming in. And soon I was to meet a guy who was to take me away from all the troubles.

CHAPTER 7

PLENTY MORE FISH

Lotus Salon was slap bang in the centre of Sunderland's shopping centre and we wanted it to work, badly. Lowis had dreams of it being so busy she'd need to take on extra staff. She'd be able to turn it into *the* beauty salon where everyone wanted to be pampered. One hundred per cent, Lowis put her heart and soul into that place, and I was just happy to be in work even though I was earning only £250 a week.

There was one big problem, though. The owner didn't have the same ambitions for Lotus as we did. In fact, he didn't give a shit about it. When I think about him now, I realise he was so dodgy. At first we had loads of supplies like waxing strips and nail varnishes, but it didn't take long for them to start running out. Lowis was on the phone each day asking for replacements and complaining everything was breaking. What first looked like a sparkly new salon was soon a shop with broken lightbulbs, plug sockets that didn't work and doors that barely hung on their hinges. The only treatment that brought customers in was the fish pedicure – Lotus was the first salon in town to offer it.

These fish were little monsters called Garra rufa that came from Turkey and chewed off the dead skin on your feet. Whatever else in that salon was broken, Lowis and I were so dedicated to taking care of those fish. I loved them. They were like rebel sharks and I'm sure I gave loads of them names!

Unlike me, Lowis was amazing at putting her foot down with customers who weren't allowed to use the fish pedicure. There was one woman who had this mingin' fungal infection, like athlete's foot, in between her toes. The minute she came in and took her shoes and socks off, I used to leg it through to the back shop. Eeeewww! I couldn't bear looking at them, so I'd always chicken out of telling her she couldn't put her gnarled hoofs into the tank. Lowis was brilliant, though, and so professional! She told her 'no' with such a straight face, but the minute that woman left, she'd run through to me and we'd piss ourselves laughing.

Soon, Sophie started coming in with her *Geordie*

Shore crew, including Charlotte, but most of the time, the salon was pretty empty. Lewis and I were so bored we used to sit chilling in the windows with our feet dangling in the tanks. I reckon the fish were bored shitless too. One day, Lewis was so bored she even shoved her face in! All the fish crowded round to chew on her cheeks – that's how much the time dragged!

We officially hit rock bottom when the upstairs loo stopped working. It was clogged up with so much poo, we even noticed some weird mould growing in the bowl. After a few weeks, it began sprouting a tree! Instead of going on a mission to the shopping centre every time we needed a wee, Lewis bought a bucket from the pound shop and we used that. It was so humiliating! Downstairs, we'd be in the therapy rooms with our clients shaping their eyebrows or waxing their legs, dressed in our neat black pinnies with perfect hair and nails, and upstairs we were pissing into a bucket!

One time we both got so desperate that we rushed upstairs together, whipped down our knickers and sat touching arse cheeks while we both weed into the bucket and our clients waited downstairs! We laughed our heads off. These poor customers had no idea what was going on behind the scenes. And, before you ask, yes, I did have a poo in the bucket. Once. And *only* once. Fortunately, I had the sense to line it with a plastic bag and then deposit the contents in the bin outside. Sorry!

We were just getting by in that place, trying to make ends meet, and having a giggle at the same time. In between our salon nightmares, Lowis and I were also going out loads. Sophie was being invited to all these fancy parties and though she didn't ask us to many, there were the odd few that we pitched up at. One night after work we joined her in a club on the Quayside called Riverside where bands played, and where we'd occasionally go dancing on club nights. Gary Beadle was there, and Sophie introduced us. I had no idea then that I would end up living with Gaz in the *Geordie Shore* house and, if I'm honest, I didn't take much notice of him. He'd turned up with a gorgeous mate. And I mean *gorgeous*! But Gaz's mate wasn't any random. He was Anthony Hutton who'd won *Big Brother* in 2005. I couldn't believe it! All throughout school I'd been glued to *Big Brother*, and I even remember one year when Nana and Grandad took me away in the caravan and I had a blazing row with Grandad because he wouldn't let me stay up to see one of the finals. According to him, there was far too much swearing and I was far too young to be watching *that programme*, which only made me want to watch it more!

Anthony had come across as dead nice on screen and, in the flesh, he was so good-looking. He had ocean blue eyes and jet black hair and the most amazing kissable lips – not that I was anywhere close to kissing them! It's not even funny how obsessed I was with him when he was on *Big Brother* – like an embarrassing fourteen-year-old girl crush. Although I was buzzing inside, I didn't want to make it that obvious. Also, Anthony was ten years older than me, so I thought, 'He's never going to be interested in me!'

After the club, we all piled back to a party in Jesmond. I was quite pissed by then so I was trying to catch his eye, brushing past him and butting in on his conversations. It worked because he came to talk to me . . . finally. But instead of me offering up some sophisticated chat, I was speechless. I was so nervous!

Anthony seemed very gentle – the polar opposite to Mark. That night I didn't even mention Mark, who was still lurking around in the background, sending me texts and wanting to meet up even though I did have another relationship with a guy called Jake after we broke up and it had been a while since we split. I felt so ashamed I'd let a boy treat me like Mark had and I didn't want Anthony to know anything about my past. Plus, we'd started to hit it off.

You're probably thinking there's a pattern here: I need the next boyfriend lined up before I leave the last one. Well, that's spot on! Even though I've always been a loner, at heart I'm a hopeless romantic. I never *want* to be single and I'm always looking for Mr Right. Anthony swept me off my feet in a kind-hearted and considerate way and I just had this feeling he'd never lay a finger on me. I couldn't believe it when he asked for my number.

'Maybe we could go out?' he said coyly.

'Er . . . yes. That would be great!'

I was trying to play it cool but inside I felt anything but. My heart was pumping.

It's so weird because the first date we ever went on was to the first screening of series one of *Geordie Shore*. It was held at Asper's Casino in Newcastle, but I could barely concentrate on the show. I was there because of Sophie, but Anthony and I couldn't keep our eyes off each other. I was besotted with him. One of the reasons I reckon Anthony and I connected was because he is from Consett, which is where I was born and is right next to Stanley. From early on, being with him felt like I'd known him all my life.

Considering the terrible experience I'd had, it didn't stop me falling in love with Anthony really quickly. I remember ringing Mam and telling her that, at last, my life was looking up. Lowis and I were working (almost!) and now I'd met the most amazing guy. With Mam, I always wanted to accentuate the positive because I knew how worried about me she was – especially with the distance between us. She's told me since that she used to wake up every day in Las

Vegas feeling so happy about Eric but so guilty about leaving me behind.

But the brilliant news was that she and Eric had decided to get married. I was made up for her! They would tie the knot in the next couple of months. But while I was excited, I knew I'd never be able to fly out to join them. Financially, I was only just keeping my head above water. Mam couldn't afford to bring me out and the bank of Nana and Grandad had been well and truly exhausted!

A few days after the ceremony, I got a DVD through the post. I watched it at Nana and Grandad's and we were all sat around like it was a proper movie. Mam and Eric didn't have a big wedding, just close friends and some of Eric's family in this cute downtown chapel. Mam's always looked lovely, but now she looked stunning. Her white silk dress was so elegant with diamanté braids all round the waist and shoulders and she held this gorgeous bouquet of white roses as she walked down the aisle. Watching that DVD was very emotional because they had written me into the vows and Eric spoke about how I couldn't be there and how I was the biggest part of Mam's life. With that, I could see Mam bubbling up. She was struggling to hold back her tears. Even Eric's bottom lip was quivering! And I was buried in the sofa at Nana's crying my eyes out. I kept wishing I'd been there for her big day, but I also felt so incredibly happy for her.

She'd done what I'd always wanted her to do – met the man of her dreams and now they were going to live happily ever after. That DVD also reminded me how much I missed Mam and how I really regretted not making the most of my stay in Las Vegas. 'Everything happens for a reason,' Nana always says, but what was the reason? I didn't know . . .

Just as I was telling Mam that my life was picking up, the salon started going completely tits up. Perhaps I tempted fate? Lowis and I soon realised our wages hadn't dropped into our bank accounts and the owner wasn't even picking up his phone. In the end, we were forced to shut up shop leaving the fish in their tanks. We felt awful. I later learned that the shopping centre manager reported the salon to the RSPCA because he'd noticed the 'Closed' sign in the window even though the fish were still swimming around. Some had already died and floated to the surface but, thankfully, the others were saved and rehomed. All these customers had bought gift vouchers for the spa too, but I doubt they ever got their money back.

At home, I wasn't getting on with me Auntie Julie, and so there I was again, moving back to Stanley to Nana and Grandad's. Arrrggghhh! It felt like I was trapped in that film *Groundhog Day*, where the actor Bill Murray lives the same day over and over. Considering I'd vowed never to go back to Stanley, it was like I couldn't get enough of the place! What made it easier this time was that although Anthony had a house in Newcastle, he was living close by in Consett. Still, I had to sign on *again* and sit through those awful jobseeker's interviews every two weeks when my caseworker would ask if I'd found work and the answer was always 'no'.

Despite Anthony having won *Big Brother*, he wasn't well off and with me back on the dole, there wasn't much we could do. One good thing was Nana and Grandad liked him, and they used to let him chill out in front of the TV and stay over. But it wasn't like I could talk to them about the weird place I was at in my head or about any of my relationships. I've never even spoken to Nana and Grandad about sex!

Not long into our relationship, Anthony and I hit a bit of a rocky patch because I couldn't seem to let go of Mark even though my awful time with him was by now long in the past. He obviously still had some kind of hold over me and I couldn't bring myself to stop speaking to him. Understandably, Anthony wasn't impressed by that at all and he laid it on the line – it was either him or Mark. 'Marnie, man! Listen to yourself!' I thought. 'You've got the most amazing guy who wants to spend time with you and treats you like a princess and you're still talking to that complete nob!' Maybe I thought Anthony was too good for me?

Having a rubbish boyfriend for so long had definitely knocked my self-esteem. Poor Anthony got the brunt of my anger. At times, it was like everything Mark had ever done welled up inside me and so when Anthony and I had arguments I was the person lashing out. On occasions, I even hit him! I was a total psycho! Plus, I was sick of living out of a suitcase with all my belongings scattered from Stanley to South Shields and Newcastle where I'd stay with mates. I didn't think of myself as homeless because I was sofa-surfing a lot of the time, and I had family who loved me, but I didn't feel settled or secure. Sadly, I think Anthony and I met each other at the wrong time. Had we been in a different place in our lives, it could have been so special because Anthony was *really* lovely.

There was also an added strain on the relationship when I fell pregnant. In the past, Mark and I had always had unprotected sex, but that had *never* happened. I was so down on myself that I'd convinced myself I could never get pregnant with Anthony either. That's how negative my mentality was. As I said, I was lashing out at Anthony, but it got to the stage where I twigged that something was wrong. My mood swings were more extreme than the pirate ship at South Shield's fair! After a while, I had this inkling that maybe I could be pregnant. It was very early days so I hadn't missed a period but something wasn't right.

'Tomorrow I'm going to do a test,' I told Anthony.

'Really?'

'There's got to be a reason I'm so psycho!'

I laughed, but I was also scared inside. The next day we were in Newcastle. On the way back from town, I was going to stop by Lowis's place to pick up some clothes, so en route I dived into Boots to pick up the kit. It felt very surreal asking for a pregnancy test, like I was having this out-of-body experience and it wasn't me standing in front of the till and paying for it.

The minute we got to Lowis's flat, I rushed through the front door while Anthony waited for me outside in the car.

'Where are you going?' Lowis looked confused as I legged it towards the bathroom.

'Just desperate for a wee,' I shouted back.

I broke open the box, pulled down my knickers, sat on the loo and weed on the stick, all the time praying I was wrong and the result would show up as negative. But it didn't. After a few minutes, I watched as the bar flashed up 'Pregnant'. My hands were shaking when I unlocked the bathroom door.

'What's wrong?' Lowis looked puzzled.

'Oh my God, Lowis, I'm pregnant!'

'Fuck!'

She stood frozen as I ran past her and back out to the car. I blurted it out to Anthony straight away, but I didn't know whether I'd done the right thing. I was nineteen and he was twenty-nine. Maybe he wanted a baby? As for me, I couldn't even get my own life sorted out, let alone look after a child!

After some thinking, it became clear that I had to have the pregnancy terminated. At the time, it felt like a very clinical decision and I don't remember feeling very emotional about it. An abortion was the only way out, and Anthony had agreed he would stand by me whatever my decision.

Because I'd been behaving so weirdly, Nana guessed too. Smoking in her house was banned, but I was chain-smoking in front of her and I didn't give a shit. And I would burst out crying for no reason. I was a blubbering lunatic! When I sat her down and told her I thought she'd go nuts, but instead she sighed and said, 'I guessed as much, pet.' That was such a relief. If she'd been angry I don't know how I would have reacted.

By the time my termination slot came around, I was six weeks pregnant, and because I was having the procedure done on the NHS, I had to spend three weeks longer being pregnant before they could fit me in. It was horrible.

One evening, Anthony and I were in Nana's front room and he knelt down and put his ear to my belly. All of a sudden, he heard this rumble. 'I don't like that,' he said. And neither did I. Both of us freaked out because we'd been trying not to think of this foetus as an actual human being.

In my heart, I knew we weren't in a position to be parents but that didn't make the termination easier. Two days before I was admitted to hospital, I had to visit the nurse who gave me one set of tablets. When I returned, they gave me a second set and that's when the cramps and bleeding started. Forget PMT at its finest; this was excruciating, and I was doubled over in bed wishing it was all over.

Nothing made me feel comfortable and I kept walking to the bathroom to check whether I'd passed the foetus. As I walked along the ward, there were a dozen beds with curtains pulled around them and girls whose faces I never saw doing exactly the same thing. It was such an eerie corridor.

When I felt everything passing through me, I couldn't even look at the bed pan at first. Eventually when the nurse checked up on me, I managed one quick glance. There was this bloody clot on the tray and I knew it was over.

Anthony was waiting outside for me, so as soon as I got cleaned up and left the ward I remember opening the car door and saying, 'Let's go.' I've never regretted choosing an abortion but I did block it out for a long time. Sometimes, usually if I'm feeling low, I do ask, 'What if?' I honestly can't imagine how my life would have turned out. I reckon if I were to get pregnant now, I'd keep the baby because I'm older and I'm in a different place in my life.

What I regret the most is putting Mam through hell. She knew all about the baby and I was ringing her and pouring my heart out every single night. I was so emotionally selfish, and it was tearing Mam apart that she wasn't with me and helping me through it.

'I'm coming home, pet,' she announced one evening.

'What?'

'I'll come first and Eric will follow.'

To this day, I have so much love and respect for Mam and the hurdles she and Eric had to jump to come home for me.

CHAPTER 8

MAM TO THE RESCUE . . . AGAIN!

Admittedly, not everyone was as positive about Mam coming home as I was. The plan was she would find work and a place to live, and Eric would follow when he'd saved enough money. Even though they were married, Eric still had to prove he could support himself if he came over to live in this country. 'They'll never find work,' Grandad kept saying. It was after the recession and everyone was finding it hard to get a job, including me, but I still kept my fingers crossed. 'She'll do it. I know she will,' I kept repeating, as if that would make it true!

The day Mam arrived back is like a sequence from one of my favourite films. Although, I'm also ashamed of myself. I was still wrapped in my own selfish world and I'd been out on an all-night bender at a place called Fever Bar on Newcastle's quayside the night before. I'd barely had any sleep and when Anthony drove me to the airport, it was typical last minute Marnie! We were so late. 'Drive faster!' I kept ordering him. Just as we were pulling in, Mam texted me to say she'd got through security. 'Where are you? I can't see you!' her message read.

With that I flew out of the front seat, shouting to Anthony to park the car and I legged it towards the sliding doors. I could see Mam standing alone by her suitcase searching for me, so I jumped the outside barrier, ran towards her and hugged her so tight. At this point, if we'd been in an actual movie, the screen would have gone all misty and an orchestra of violins would have reached a crescendo. 'I'm so glad you're home,' I kept repeating. Mam was back. I'd waited so long to see her and now she was finally here. I couldn't take it in. The worst thing was I was even thinner than I'd been in Las Vegas. She didn't mention anything, but I watched her staring at my arms and shoulders. Now she remembers gulping at the sight of me. At that moment, she says, she knew she'd made the right decision.

Even though Mam was home, we couldn't be with each other all the time. She couldn't stay with Nana and Grandad, so she ended up moving back in with her mam in Stanley. As much as it was awful for me to be back in Stanley, it was a killer for Mam. She'd spent so long when I was a kid trying to get me out of there. But she was confident and really determined that she was going to sort our lives out. She had this unstoppable drive! And, she did it! She actually did it!

Anthony was amazing, too. Because Mam didn't drive, he took her to loads of job interviews. Then, one day she came back so excited because she'd been offered a job at Nobles amusement arcade in South Shields. Downstairs, all the roulette tables and fruit machines were in one room, but upstairs they'd offered her work as a cashier in the tanning salon. 'Well done, Mam!' I kept saying. I was dead proud of her. That job was all she needed to get us back to South Shields and put a deposit down on a flat. We found a place and agreed to rent it for £600 a month, which was a lot of money for Mam. But the amazing thing was she didn't ask me for a penny. Naturally, I wanted to pay my way somehow, so I asked if I could help out Sophie's Dad at Mambos because Sophie was now living the high life with *Geordie Shore*. The job wasn't great. I was working for my Uncle Kevin behind the bar serving drinks and earning £30 a shift, but at least it was *something*.

I loved our new flat despite it being in Chichester, which is quite a rough area of South Shields. There were two bedrooms on the top floor for me, Mam and

Eric and it had a large sitting room and kitchen on the middle floor. But I couldn't help thinking what Mam had given up to come home. She'd always been thin but since she'd been living in the States she'd gained weight and she looked so happy. Now she was back to crap weather and worrying whether Eric would ever make it to the UK. Eric is officially my hero, though. So he could save enough money to make the trip, he sold his car and started using his bike to get to work. It took him months to get the money together, but he did it. When he landed, Mam was over the moon. Automatically, we became this little unit – the three musketeers!

Soon Eric had found a job building parts for cars, and with Mam also working, I wanted it to be my turn to get a break in life. I wanted that sooooo badly, but I was starting to feel like a cat running out of lives! Especially when some unwelcome visitors turned up on the doorstep.

Mam and Eric had both gone to work and I was still at home. My shifts at Mambos didn't start until the early evening, so I often had the day to myself to sloth around the flat. When the doorbell went, I assumed it was the postman, and I'm sure I was still in my pyjamas when I opened the door. Standing right in front of me were two policemen in uniform. Shit! My mind was racing. It's Mam. She's dead! Where's Eric? What the fuck is going on?

'Are you Marnie Simpson?' one of them stared at me.

'Yes,' I gulped.

'We're here to arrest you on a charge of fraud.'

'Whaaaaaat the hell?'

I was totally floored. And I actually had *no idea* what this officer was talking about.

'We'd like you to accompany us to the station. You do not have to say anything . . . Anything you do say may be given in evidence . . .'

'You can't!' I pleaded with them. 'I've got work and I haven't done anything wrong.'

Thankfully, the officers gave me time to get dressed, but I was still protesting my innocence as I stepped into the back of the police car. My head was spinning because I still didn't know what I was being accused of. The last time I'd come into contact with 'the authorities' was the time I was twelve and I stole the pizza but, if anything, that was just ridiculous and funny. This, on the other hand, was deadly serious!

By the time I was escorted into the interview room, I was a mess. The officers kept asking me where I was on 19 August 2009 . . . 'How should I know?' I said sarcastically. 'I can't even remember what I did last week!' Then they asked me if I'd been in a car that had collided with a load of lads in a minibus going to Edinburgh. 'No!' I said forcefully. They went on to describe an accident that had apparently happened near the Tyne Tunnel, but I was blank. 'Me?' I kept saying. 'I don't know anything!'

It turned out that apparently I'd been a passenger in a Peugeot being driven by a guy called Ben Le Blond. He was a lad I'd known for years from South Shields, but I hadn't seen him for ages and I sure as hell hadn't been with him in the car that day. I was later to find out that he and the lads in the minibus had damaged the vehicles earlier and then staged a pile-up so they could claim for whiplash injuries. But because there were so many of them, the insurance bill had come to more than £134,000 and that's when suspicions had been aroused. Although the 'accident' happened in 2009, the insurers didn't prosecute until two years later, by which time they had a dossier proving all the lads knew each other and it was a massive scam.

Ben, who'd already fled the scene by the time the cops showed up, had claimed for himself and me so he could get double the money. I was fucking furious that I'd been dragged into something I had no involvement with. Nevertheless, the cops had my false claim in front of them and so I was charged with fraud with all these other charvas, most of whom I didn't even know. I'd have to stand trial. 'What the hell are Mam and Nana and Grandad going to say?'

Mam being Mam was so supportive. As I say, that woman has so much love for me, it's crazy. I didn't even have to argue my case. OK, I'd been in trouble before, but even Mam knew I wasn't capable of this crime.

Maybe it was coincidence, or maybe someone was watching over me, but just as all that kicked off, an advert to apply for *Geordie Shore* popped up on my Facebook. With no job, on bail and with a court case pending, I thought, 'Why the hell not? I've got nothing to lose! Why shouldn't I see if I'm good enough?'

The more I thought about it, the more I wanted to try doing what Sophie had done. If there's one thing I had going for me, it was my personality. *Geordie Shore* didn't care about qualifications, and Sophie had told me it was all about how you came across on camera.

If I'm brutally honest, I knew if I told Sophie she would be upset. Despite being at that screening of the first series of *Geordie Shore* at Aspers Casino, and a couple of parties, Sophie had kept me at arms' length. She had her 'celebrity *Geordie Shore*' friends and me and she'd made it clear that her TV life was 'her thing' and I was excluded from it. I guess I didn't want to look desperate by stepping into her shoes so I was secretive about applying. I didn't even tell Anthony, I was that sly. Every time he came into the room and I was on the laptop, I'd slam it shut. The thing was, I *was* desperate. I didn't have *anything* going for me, but I did feel embarrassed clinging to Sophie's world.

The producers were auditioning for series four, and there hadn't been any new housemates since Ricci Guarniccio and Rebecca Walker in series two. So Sophie kept telling me that rumours were flying around there'd be someone new soon. It was sooooo hard not to tell her I'd filled out the application form and sent it off. Every time I almost blurted it out, I had to bite my tongue. Only Mam knew, and when I got a call in the Autumn of 2011 asking me to go to the audition in Newcastle, I couldn't believe it! It was like I'd waited my whole life for this moment. I was shaking, but inside I thought, 'Yessss! I'm going to give it my all.'

Mam came with me to the initial interview at the Royal Station Hotel in Newcastle, and that felt very strange. The last time I'd been sat in a hotel lobby it had been with Sophie on her audition and I hadn't even been allowed to enter the room. Now it was me in front of one producer. That day is such a haze, I don't even remember the woman who interviewed me! I was so terrified, I'd stopped on the way with Mam to buy a miniature bottle of vodka to neck beforehand, which seemed to give me the false confidence I needed.

There was a whole string of questions like, 'What are you like? How wild are you? What do you do on a night out? What are your relationships like? What kind of housemate will you be?' In response, I was giving it the big 'un, saying that I loved getting mortal and flirting with boys. I didn't give a fuck what people thought of me, and I'd need way longer than an hour to tell her about my mad relationships! The funny thing was, I was probably more reserved than any of the others. If I'm honest, I reckon they were interested in me purely because I was Sophie's cousin and they knew how me entering the house might play out on screen.

On the way home, Mam gave me a big speech, saying, 'You're definitely going to get it.' I wasn't so sure, and I was particularly uncertain because on the application form I'd had to declare if I had any criminal convictions or court cases pending. With the whole fraud thing hanging over me, I'd had to be honest.

I went from oscillating between thinking that this could be my big break to imagining a life signing on or doing shitty restaurant jobs. The worst thing was that not long after, *Geordie Shore* rang me saying how much they'd loved me, but they couldn't take my application further because I was on bail. It was just as I'd expected. I was devastated. Any dreams I had of quitting my job and making something of myself ended right there. 'Maybe I am so shit life's not supposed to work out for me,' I thought.

Perhaps it was my state of mind that put an end to mine and Anthony's relationship, too. Since I'd moved back to South Shields with Mam, we'd drifted apart and we weren't seeing each other half as much. I have only lovely things to say about Anthony now, and there is a part of me that does wonder what would have happened if we'd stayed together. If I'd stayed with him would I ever have got on *Geordie Shore*? Maybe I'd have two kids and no hope of leaving South Shields like a lot of my friends from home. Whatever crazy shit I was messed up in, I was still determined to do something with my life, I just didn't know what.

Just before me and Anthony split for good, I put myself in for the annual Miss Newcastle contest. It was obvious I wasn't going to realise my TV ambition but now I knew MTV had loved me, I reckoned I was still in with a chance of doing something, even if it wasn't *that*.

To enter the competition, I had to fill out an application and if I got through to the next stage, I'd be called for a photoshoot. Instead of thinking I'd get anywhere, I approached it like a little hobby, playing it down in my head to avoid the same disappointment. It worked!

When I look back on those photos now, I cringe. There's one of me in this zipped up bralette looking like my hair's been dragged through a hedge backwards. Then there's another where I've clearly overdone it on the fake tan. I look like a Belisha beacon! The last one is all sultry and soft focus like I was pretending to be Kate Winslet leaning against the bow of the *Titanic* with Leonardo DiCaprio holding onto me. If only!

Whatever Miss Newcastle was, it was loads of fun. Alongside twenty other girls, I had to learn how to catwalk properly – which, let me tell you, in lingerie and a pair of stilettos is bloody hard! The other girls in the competition were all gorgeous and, unlike I'd expected, they weren't bitchy at all. Maybe some of them saw the competition as the stepping stone to the Miss England finals, but most of us were there to have fun. I still keep in touch with some of the girls. They were a right laugh to be around.

The theme for the main event was the 2012 Olympics so we had to pose with a Union Jack as well as strut our stuff in the opening sequence with Olympic flags from all around the world. We spent *ages* learning that routine. Being a black-tie event and attended by so many people, it was really nerve-wracking. I was well out of my comfort zone! Backstage, we could hear the song 'We Found Love' by Rihanna blare from the speakers and that was the cue for our grand entrance. Apart from shitting myself that I was going to tumble arse over tit on the runway, it was plain sailing. We all took a deep breath and held onto each other tightly. And, once I was out there, I enjoyed every moment. I loved that the crowd was clapping and cheering us on.

As the night went on the judges marked us in three different categories: evening wear, lingerie and swimwear. Unsurprisingly, I didn't win, but I did get into the top ten, which I was dead chuffed about. It made me even more frustrated that the whole *Geordie Shore* dream had turned out to be just that: a dream. However much I tried, I couldn't get my looming court case off my mind.

On the morning of my appearance at Newcastle Crown Court, Mam and Eric took time off work to come with me. I didn't even need to ask! The problem was that in my head, I had so many life plans. I was terrified I'd enter court an innocent person and end up with a custodial sentence. That could seriously mess up my future. Apart from worrying about the outcome, it did feel good that I could go in there with my head held high. Everybody knew I'd done nowt wrong and if Mam, Eric and my family were behind me then that gave me the courage to be strong and brave.

As soon as we arrived, my solicitor talked me through some of the procedure. It all felt so formal, like I was on trial for my life. Intense is the only way I can describe it! Once I was ushered into the court room, I had to stand far away from Mam and Eric who were in the viewing gallery. It felt so awkward having to sit with all these lads and I kept meeting Mam's eyes, just to reassure myself she was there.

At times, though, Mam was grinning from ear to ear. She wasn't taking it seriously *at all*! She almost made me burst out laughing! Some of the lads were proper wrong 'uns and every time one of them got up to speak she started making these awful faces, like she'd swallowed a wasp. They were proper Geordie charvas with trackie bottoms and trainers and full-on tattoos, and between them they could hardly string a sentence together.

Ben was now working off-shore in the oil industry and clearly earning a bit of money seeing as he'd turned up in a sharp grey suit and a black shirt. We spoke briefly. I asked him why he'd involved me in the scam, but I didn't get an answer. He looked more embarrassed than anything. Thank God that when the judge read out the verdicts, I did not get a suspended sentence like the others. Instead, I was handed a community order which was a non-custodial sentence.

Naturally, I was pissed off I'd been handed anything. But, 150 hours' voluntary work in a charity shop, which is what I ended up doing, was a lot less terrifying than being banged up aged twenty-one! Jeeezzz, that work dragged. I was made to tag clothes in a YMCA charity shop in South Shields and I'm sure they hated me. Every time I turned up, I had a face like a wet weekend and I never stayed for more than an hour. That voluntary work took so long. I thought I was going to die waiting for it to finish. What I didn't know was that my life was about to turn a corner . . .

CHAPTER 9

GEORDIE SHORE, HERE I COME!

In between seeing out my community service, I was still working at my Uncle Kevin's restaurant, wishing I was anywhere else. Honestly, I do believe I have a guardian angel watching over me. Whenever my life has been at rock bottom, someone's always stepped in out of the blue and saved me. I guess I must have done something right in a previous life! This time my angel wasn't Mam or Lowis; it was a woman called Nia.

One evening around February time in 2013, I'd just finished my six-hour shift at Mambos. The weather was freezing, plus it was dark and pissing down with rain. By the time I reached home I looked like a drowned rat! Then a message popped up on my

Facebook: 'Hi Marnie. Just wanted to know if you're still interested in taking part in *Geordie Shore*?' Nia had written, explaining that she was a director on the show.

'My court case is over, so yeah!' I replied straightaway.

'Mam! *Geordie Shore* just messaged me!' I started screaming.

'They haven't, have they?'

From that moment on my life felt like it was rushing at 100 miles an hour! The very next morning I got another message asking me if I could get to London by that afternoon! Whaaaaaat?

I'd just got out of the shower. My hair was sopping wet, but I thought, 'Yesss! This is my only chance and I can't blow it.' I threw on some clothes, any clothes, phoned a cab and took the next train from Newcastle.

I'd never even been to London on my own before. I felt like a fish out of water. On the journey down, I even convinced myself the show would end soon anyway, so maybe there wasn't any point going in. Then I predicted that if I did get in the housemates and the public would hate me and I'd only last one series. All that negativity and doubt!

I needed to be at Lime Pictures, the company that produce the show, by three p.m., where I was introduced to the show's executive producer and commissioner – Kate Bates and Jake Attwell. It was their first series on *Geordie Shore* and to this day, I love them both. I think they could see I was shitting myself and from the get-go they put me at ease.

Immediately, I felt this bond with Kate. She had long blonde hair and was very pretty and dead friendly. It was like talking to a second mam, she was so caring. Jake had long hair and the cheekiest grin and from that moment I always had a little crush on him.

We ran through the same questions I'd answered in the initial audition, but the way they were talking it was like I'd got it already.

'When you are in the house, how are you going to deal with Sophie?' Kate asked.

'She'll be fine. She's me cousin! Why wouldn't she be happy?'

Admittedly, I was playing a bit dumb. At the end of the chat they repeated that they liked me, but if I did get on the show there was to be a number one rule: Sophie must know nothing about it. I knew they were taking a massive risk because there had only ever been one other girl parachuted into the house and that had been Rebecca Walker who didn't last one series. Sophie had told me she'd swanned in like she owned the place, which was never going to go down well with the strong personalities in there. So I understood introducing me could be a disaster. Plus, I knew more than ever that Sophie would want to kill me. But me being me, I put that to the back of my mind. You could say I was in denial! If Sophie had understood what a bad place I was in in my life before *Geordie Shore*, she probably would have been happy for me. That said, I never wanted to admit to her just how shit my life was. Had the tables been turned, I'm sure I would have been pleased for Sophie, but as my debut in the house edged closer, I felt awful.

Sophie had just come back from a tour of Australia and that feeling got worse when we went for a sunbed together. She was buzzing about the trip, despite being knackered from all the filming. And she was moaning there wasn't enough gap between Australia and filming for the next series, which was just about to start.

'Oh, really?' I said. *Shit!* I hadn't had confirmation, but that was the series I was due to appear in! I was trying so hard not to give the game away.

'I'm sure they're going to bring someone else into the house . . .'

'Maybe they will.'

I was squirming inside. I *hated* lying to Sophie, but the reality was she and I had led different lives. Sophie's never had to struggle. She's always had what's she wanted. When she was seventeen and she passed her driving test, her dad bought her a car the next day – that's how spoiled she was!

Even though I didn't get the green light until two

days before I went in, both Mam and I knew *Geordie Shore* was finally going to happen. In the run-up, the crew asked to film at Mam's flat so they could compile my backstory. They would never have done that if I wasn't going in. Mam nearly died! We were filmed upstairs while I was packing my suitcase. And, naturally, the producers wanted us to concentrate on how Sophie was going to react when I stepped through the door.

'Just go in there and be yourself; you're beautiful,' Mam kept saying to me.

I didn't feel that beautiful, though. With no money, I'd not bought a show-stopping outfit. Instead, I had this plain black Primark vest top that I wore as a dress, and an old trilby hat I used to wear out clubbing. Mam says now that when I left and she tidied up my room, she was struck by how few clothes I owned. I had a tiny £10-suitcase that was falling apart, and I'd taken everything with me!

My introduction was filmed in the studio, which was a weird experience. I'd heard Sophie banging on about 'green screen' but I couldn't imagine what it felt like. Basically, you sit in front of a green cloth chatting shit to a camera, and then the graphics are projected on afterwards. It's so part of my routine now, I don't even think about it, although I do find the whole process really awkward and boring.

Green screen is completed in our breaks when we're

not doing tasks, or after the series ends. Filming can go on for hours, and I find it impossible to sit there on a stool for that long. The one great thing is that you can let rip about the housemates if there's been an argument or someone's doing your head in. Or you can just be really stupid. There's what's called a logger on the show who takes down everything that's been said, so if you do dry up, the producer can remind you of stuff you've done or a specific conversation or something that's happened in the house, and you follow on with your reaction.

I'm probably the worst at green screen. Sometimes I do my lines more than thirteen times to get them right! At first I used to be there for nine hours, but I've got it down to around four now. People like Charlotte are naturally hilarious, but I'm often tired or pissed off or just not feeling energetic and funny. But even then, I'm fussy about which people I like doing it with and I'll ask for certain producers. I like the ones that make me feel relaxed because when I first started I was so uncomfortable that I'd sweat all the way through.

I was also keen not to come across as fake. Some people do, don't they? After a few practices, my first words to the camera were, 'I'm Marnie. I'm twenty. I'm a natural beauty. Real boobs. Real hair and a really good arse.' I'd say that was me in a nutshell!

Apart from the Sophie situation, what I found hardest about entering *Geordie Shore* was that I couldn't accept something good was happening to me. Since Sophie had started in *Geordie Shore*, it had moved from trendy Jesmond to a warehouse in a business park in Wallsend. Eric drove me to the house and spinning around my head for the whole journey was the question, 'How the *hell* have I got *here*?' Self doubt was eating me up! So, Marnie did the sensible thing and got mortal on vodka coke in a pub round the corner. Even Eric said I was going for it, but it was the only way I could calm my nerves.

'I love you and I'll see you soon.' I gave Eric a sloppy, drunken hug when we arrived.

'Just go in there and have a ball.'

Eric was such a reassuring and steady person that I almost wished he was coming in with me. I felt sad to leave him.

The minute the car dropped me off at around seven p.m., I was on my own. Armed with my tatty suitcase, I took a deep breath and opened the door. 'Hi!' I shouted. All I remember was seeing Scott Timlin and Gary's shocked faces. '*It's Marnie!*' They were buzzing because they knew me as Sophie's baby cousin and from going out in Newcastle. Their reaction made me feel so bewildered that I fell over the step! I couldn't believe it! My first appearance on

TV and I'd completely fucked it up! And when I say 'bewildered' I mean 'palatic'.

Sophie legged it downstairs and rushed towards me; I could see she was in shock. What she didn't understand was that I was never there to cause trouble, but I did feel embarrassed. From the moment I arrived I was desperate to take her aside and say, 'I'm here and I'm sorry and I hope you're going to be OK.' It didn't take long for the cracks to show.

Admittedly, it is hard being a newbie in the *Geordie Shore* house, especially as I entered alone. All the housemates had been together since the beginning and friendships had been made and broken. I expected it to be tough, but not as tough as it turned out to be. From the beginning, the girls were stand-offish and I felt like they were all slagging me off behind my back. Scott and Gary, on the other hand, were so welcoming and on my first night, I stuck to them like glue.

Anyone who knows me knows I enjoy having a flirt but each time I went near them it was like Sophie, Charlotte and Holly Hagan were burning a hole in the back of my head. That was disappointing because I'd met Charlotte on nights out in town and I thought she was mint. Funnily, the only person who was nice to me that night was Vicky Pattison, which still makes me laugh considering how fake she turned out to be. But more of that later!

Back in the house, Sophie kept whispering in my

ear to stay away from the boys. At the time, I naively thought she was being protective towards me, but I wised up. Sophie didn't want me in *Geordie Shore* and if I got with one of the lads then there was more chance of the producers keeping me in for another series. At the time, I had no idea about how TV worked.

I feel bad saying this because Sophie's my cousin and I love her, but I'm sure she would admit that she was spiteful back then. We've been through a lot since and all I can say is that girl's done a lot of growing up. We both have. Blood is thicker than water and our relationship is completely different now. She's told me since that it *was* difficult for the girls. They couldn't automatically be bitches to me because I was Sophie's baby cousin. And she didn't know whether to look after me or hate me. Arrrggghhh!

No joke, during my debut series there were times when I wanted to sack it all off and walk out. But Mam's probably the only person who knows what a determined person I am. The more the girls griefed me the more I thought, 'I'm staying in this house whether you like it or not!'

Holly Hagan didn't make any secret of the fact she hated me from day one. Her and Scott had a history together but there wasn't anything going on between them by the time I arrived. I mean, they weren't having sex! I didn't even like Scott at first, but it didn't take long for me to warm to him because he has these amazing blue eyes and he is funny and friendly and, most importantly, he was *single*. As far as I could work out, Holly and I weren't going to be friends and she wasn't in a position to dictate who Scott could get with. Did I feel I was breaking any girl code if I went there with him? No! All I thought was, 'This guy's giving me fanny flutter and I've only just got here!'

Ask me how I feel about that now, and I'd say the total opposite. In fact, when series seven finally aired, I had loads of friends round to Mam's to watch it and I was mortified. From the minute I entered the house, I found myself pure cringe, and I spent most of the time with my head buried in my hands. 'Is that what I go on like?' I asked Mam. It was a real eye-opener and also very strange because I had this perception of myself that clearly wasn't true. I like the boys but I was way out of control. It was like I'd regenerated as some turbo-charged Marnie! In one scene I was even in the upstairs bedroom flashing my arse cheeks to Scott and Gary! As if that wasn't bad enough, I bent over to pick up my hat and the guys had a clear view right up my fanny. 'I'm a complete fruit!' I thought. But I guess if I wasn't the producers wouldn't have liked me.

On my first night, we hit Florita's Bar. Whereas before I'd only ever been a bystander watching Sophie being filmed in a club, I had to keep pinching myself that this time it was me in the series! But what viewers don't realise is just how long it takes getting in and out of a club. The crew keep you in the taxi for *ages* while they set up all the cameras. You can't even smoke a tab! From the outset, I've always found that draining and I've never got used to being told what I can and cannot do.

Whatever happened that night, I vowed I was going to be my fun self but I couldn't help noticing that Holly ignored me the whole night. There was only one thing for it! I carried on dancing and getting mortal with the others. OK, guilty as charged, I may have been grinding my arse on Scott's lap, but I didn't see Scott complaining! That seemed to tip Sophie over the edge. She started giving me a lecture on how I was going to upset every girl in the house. But not one of those girls had made me feel welcome. I openly agreed with Sophie to her face, but underneath I thought, 'I'm doing what the hell I want.'

Back at the house, Holly and I did try to clear the air, but nothing she said made the blindest bit of difference. One minute she was telling me how she didn't care if me and Scott got together, but her face was saying the complete opposite! When Scott did come into my room later that night and we did kiss, I didn't even touch his willy! It was all very innocent and despite being mortal, the truth was I actually felt very shy about kissing anyone on TV. Scott *was* a dead good kisser, though. Ten out of ten. But, thank fuck he didn't stay, because within minutes I started spewing my guts up, like I always do. I'd upset the girls, kissed a boy and projectile vomited all in the space of eight hours. Welcome to *Geordie Shore*, Marnie!

What I soon realised was that being cooped up in that house makes everyone go a bit cuckoo. And anyone who claims they're unaware the cameras are filming is bare-faced lying. First of all, we have an actual cameraman following us around – except in the shag pad where there's a fixed camera. Even then, you *do* know. As I discovered when I was later to appear on *Celebrity Big Brother*; however much you kid yourself that the cameras aren't rolling, you are aware that they are. If you have a sneaky conversation, you're always thinking, 'Can I get away with it?'

As well as getting used to the weirdness of TV, the intense heat of all the girls griefing me was driving me mental. I needed to calm the situation, and fast. So I decided that even though I liked Scott, I would stay clear of him. Well, that was an epic fail! While my opinion of the girls was getting lower, the chemistry between us was getting hotter. It's like when you stop eating chocolate and then that's all you ever think about! Even though by my third night in the house we did end up spooning in bed, no one believes Scott and I have only ever kissed. I know he fancied me, though, because he'd always have a proper radgie if he saw me and Gary chatting.

'What happened to staying away, Marnie?' Sophie grilled me.

As much as I denied that anything had happened, I thought, 'They hate me anyway so I might as well crack on.'

On screen, Sophie gave me the big guilt trip saying I had to choose between my family and Scott. My family? And Scott? I thought, 'Calm down, Sophie. It's not life or death. I'm only necking on with a lad!'

Off camera, it was even worse. There were times when I'd be sat there on my own while the girls – including Sophie – were in a huddle giggling. Holly may have described me as 'thin and pretty' and said she felt intimidated by me when she was interviewed in green screen later, but I was taken aback by her comment. Those girls were *really* intimidating and the boys were terrified of them. They dominated that house. Vicky in particular was such a forceful character. It was like living with a she-man! She needed to be in control of everybody.

Sometimes I had to walk out to cry and then I'd be too scared to walk back in. A producer would spend ages talking me down.

'I hate those girls. They hate me. I want my phone, and I want to see Mam.'

'Marnie, you're brilliant, we want you in the house . . .'

Every time they managed to persuade me back. But, being new to TV and being in that environment felt very surreal and I couldn't help getting lost in the bubble of it all. To give Scott his dues, he did take me aside and give me the best advice: 'Look. You come in here. It's just a show. You get on with it. You have a laugh, and you leave and see your own family and friends,' he said. The problem was, I really needed *Geordie Shore* and it *was* real to me. It took me ages to realise that this was *only TV*.

I had to face facts, though. The close bond between the housemates that Sophie had experienced wasn't happening for me, and soon it wasn't happening between me and Scott either. While I was wondering whether he still fancied me, Scott had other plans. On one night, he necked on with another lass while we were out. But he'd definitely met his match with Marnie because two can play at that game! When I learned later that he'd wanted to test the water by making me jealous, I thought that was pathetic. Then I got home to find him balls deep in the shag pad with the same random he'd picked up. Obviously, that was going to get me furious. It was time for Marnie to do some serious cock-blocking. I had no hesitation about flinging open the door and giving the happy couple the third degree. 'What are you doing in here? Have you two had sex?' Talk about a passion killer!

Meanwhile, Sophie had got herself into a right state over me and Scott. I couldn't understand why she was so bothered. I felt sad because I wanted us to be close. The producers had even arranged for Sophie's boyfriend Joel to turn up to cheer her up. I'd not met Joel before. His Essex accent was a bit weird, but secretly I liked that instead of him automatically taking Sophie's side, he said to both of us, 'You're family. You should stick together.'

With Joel around everything felt calmer. Scott and I, and Joel and Sophie even went on a double date. But later when we got to House of Smith, the whole night got very messy and Vicky ended up getting mortal and throwing a stiletto heel at someone after an ice bucket was chucked over her. Her shoe landed in two girls' faces. One of them was a bouncer and the other was an eighteen-year-old model who needed stitches afterwards. Now, I'm a hothead and if pushed, I'll definitely have a bit of a scraffle. But Vicky has a wicked temper. The worst thing was, no one knew who threw the ice. In a drunken diva moment, Vicky just lashed out. Suddenly, security were on her and dragging her out of the club.

We were also sent home immediately and told to get to bed. Sometimes in the house you do feel like a naughty schoolgirl being punished for truanting off school! Months later, Vicky ended up having to go to court on two charges of assault and came out with a fine and community service.

For me, the whole evening felt very shocking and I remember just standing there thinking, *What the hell?* I knew I wasn't popular in the house so it was a reminder that the atmosphere could switch at any point. After that the producers activated an immediate break in the filming, which was a relief because I got my phone back and I was able to ring Mam. It was so nice to hear her voice.

But later in the series, Sophie left too. None of us had a clue why she'd gone because, unlike Vicky, we didn't see her argue with anyone on a night out. Instead, on Holly's twenty-first birthday, Sophie left a note on her bed saying she'd had to leave to sort some things out and she wasn't coming back.

I automatically assumed she and Joel had problems and it wasn't until later we realised she'd been booted off for a racist comment that she'd apparently made to someone in a club. Whatever Sophie is, she's not a racist. First off, all her own family are foreign because Sophie's dad's from Iran, but I also didn't believe Sophie would say the N-word to anyone.

I was struggling to understand what had gone on and I genuinely felt gutted she wasn't going to be in the show for the foreseeable future. On the morning of Holly's birthday, when Anna – our on-screen boss who runs Tash-On Tours and sends us to work – came to tell us that she didn't know when Sophie would be coming back, it put such a downer on the day. I assumed the housemates would secretly blame me, given that Sophie and I had not seen eye-to-eye since I entered the show.

I can't help thinking now that her being unhappy prompted her drunken rant. But, even more gutting was that Sophie leaving was to destroy our relationship for more than a year.

Some people call it chaos – I call it family!

CHAPTER 10

BEADLE'S ABOUT

I hadn't been out of the *Geordie Shore* house two minutes and my life had changed in so many different ways. Not all of them good . . .

Social media was something I was definitely not prepared for. It's a feeding frenzy! By the time series seven aired, trolls were giving me a really hard time, calling me a slag for the way Scott and I had carried on. Funnily, he didn't receive the same level of abuse. What is it with girls, huh?

And loads of people had started commenting on how I looked; for example that I had a big nose. I found those comments hard to ignore, and I'm convinced they played a massive part in me eventually having plastic surgery.

I still find social media difficult. This year, when my then boyfriend Lewis and I split up after he'd been exposed cheating, Twitter went nuts and I realised there's nothing you can do to stop it or control it. I've even had some bloke messaging me saying he's crazy about me and whenever he sees pictures of me kissing people, it's like I've driven a stake through his heart. I've never even met the guy! These days, I take a deep breath. Who are these people who are so sad that all they want to do is spend their time either slagging me off or falling in love with me? Bonkers!

It wasn't all bad, though. First of all, I must have been doing something right because the ratings for series seven were the best they'd ever been. When the producers told me, I was absolutely over the moon because it made all the pain worthwhile.

Secondly, before I'd gone into the house, Mam and I had talked about her moving from Chichester to a nicer area, especially now Eric was permanently in South Shields and they were both working. Down by the harbour, there is a lovely little secluded development that I loved. Mam had been searching online in case a place came up, but I couldn't believe it when I got out and she told me they'd already moved into a two-bedroom apartment while I'd been filming. By the time I arrived, they'd kitted out my bedroom and it felt brilliant to be back in our little unit again.

One of my other highlights was going to Topshop and being able to buy a jumper I loved. OK, I know that sounds proper daft, but I'd never been able to do that before. I'd always been getting by on my dole money or wages and this was the first time I'd been properly paid. And, of course, I bought Elvis, my naughty dog.

Going out was much more fun, too. Nothing could beat that feeling of partying late at a club and not getting stranded because I'd spent my taxi fare home. And I could pay for my friends. Admittedly, I *knew* some of them were cling-on friends – there because I was paying and I could get them into all the clubs – but I didn't care. For a while I turned into this mad spender, and it's only recently that I've had a massive wake-up call. What's the point in earning good money if all you do is piss it up the wall?

A day or so after I came home, another surprise was waiting for me – a text from Gary Beadle. All the time Scott and I had been dancing around each other in the house, I'd not really twigged that Gaz had wanted in on the action. *Can I come over and see you?* the text read. I thought, why not? If Gaz was breaking any lad code with Scott then that was his problem. Anyhow, what Scott didn't know wouldn't hurt him.

With hindsight, I don't think I ever *fancied* Gary. Instead, I wanted to go there out of curiosity. He and Charlotte had had this dramatic on–off romance before I'd even entered the show but it wasn't like they were boyfriend and girlfriend. And I was yet to clock that although now I love Gary Beadle to bits, he is the biggest fanny rat on the planet. Still, that afternoon all I wanted to do was take him into my bed and have sex with him. As I say, after six weeks in the house wondering whether Scott and I would ever neck on, Gary's willy suddenly seemed very attractive.

Charlotte had always joked that Gary had the biggest penis – The Parsnip as she named it. And she was not wrong! No joke, it was literally as big as my forearm. I was scared of it! What I hadn't predicted was how dirty Gaz would be. If you want filthy sex, then Gary Beadle's your man; but a loving boyfriend? No way! I don't think Gaz is even capable of love. And the sex with Gary went on waaayyy too long. I mean, *for hours*. No foreplay. No cuddles. Just in and out *for an eternity*. Considering I have the concentration span of a goldfish, this was not ideal. He was so full-on, too. For example, he'd spit on us and chuck us off the bed. I thought, 'Who the hell are you? Some hot-shot porn star?'

It didn't stop us seeing each other. In between series seven and eight, Gary and I hooked up a couple of times, but only for sex. Obviously, that made everything so much more complicated when we eventually did go back into the house. No one knew, and we'd made a pact to keep it secret.

While I was dead chuffed to be asked back by MTV for another series, I was also incredibly scared about how I would be received in the house. Other than Gary, I didn't see anyone from *Geordie Shore* in between filming. I didn't even miss anyone either because no one, other than the lads, had made me feel welcome. Before I walked in, I thought, 'These girls have put me through hell. Just go in there and smash it, Marnie.'

I was also very sad that Sophie would not be joining me. I wanted our relationship to be OK, but even I could not have predicted her exit from the last series. She'd made it obvious how bitter and angry she was about my arrival and her having to leave. I got a few texts from Sophie during the break that were quite abusive; telling me I should leave the show and that I wasn't going to make anything of myself. One even read that if I'd been desperate for money she would have given it to me. We've never spoken about it, but I know Sophie didn't mean to be so nasty. Her whole world had come crashing down and she was lashing out in frustration. I did feel hurt by those texts because I knew I wasn't a horrible person and I hadn't gone out of my way to treat Sophie badly, despite what she and the girls might have thought.

As it turned out, when I made it inside not one person was there to welcome me. The only girl I could find was Holly bouncing up and down on a waterbed that had been installed in the shag pad. The second I saw it, I envisioned World War III breaking out over who was going to christen it. I didn't realise it would actually be me! Especially as my first words to Holly were: 'I'm staying away from the boys. I want to have fun with the girls this time. That's my priority.' Yeah right! Pull the other one, Marnie!

This time around we had no idea which housemates would be joining us. After the fight in the club it was unclear whether Vicky would return and I, personally, wouldn't have cared either way. Vicky had been friendly, but as I've said before, I found her very controlling. Whenever she walked into a room, I could automatically feel myself backing off because she'd have a snide comment to make and she'd always be armed with a bitchy comeback. Even now, I don't believe that the friendships she had with the other girls were real. At a push, Holly got on with Vicky, but the rest I'd call 'frenemies' – they all pretended to like her, but underneath I reckoned Charlotte and Sophie resented her because whether anyone liked it or not, Vicky ruled the roost, and those girls were so competitive.

Charlotte had also won *Big Brother* in between series seven and eight and so we didn't know whether she'd want to come back. Back then, I couldn't believe the public had actually voted for her! All I kept thinking was, 'She's been such a bitch to me, and then she goes and wins that!' It's funny to think how much I hated those girls and what brilliant friends we've all become. They all spoke about the 'Geordie Shore family', but in series eight I knew I was still not part of it.

My only chink of hope was when James Tindale turned up with his girlfriend Kate, who I'd met in the last series and who I'd really bonded with. Kate was dead friendly and a great laugh. As a joke, she arrived alongside James, who announced, 'Meet our new housemate!'

'Hallelujah!' I was doing cartwheels in my head. 'At last, a girl I like!'

Holly's face, on the other hand, looked more like a melted welly. She despised Kate, not only because she was tall and brunette and drop-dead gorgeous, but because James and Holly had had sex eons ago, which was the same possessive shit she'd tried on with me and Scott. Get over it, girl!

From the off I found James a lovely, steady, normal lad. He was well into Kate and his gym and being healthy and I think that's why he only lasted until series ten. He grew out of appearing in the programme. And you do have to be a complete nutbag to keep going back to Geordie Shore. James just wasn't like that. Neither was he a complete fanny rat like Gaz and Scott.

My bubble soon burst, though, when it turned out

that Kate entering the house was a practical joke dreamed up by the producers.

People also ask me what it feels like to have sex on national TV, and I still don't know the answer. All I can say is I've *never* had good sex in the *Geordie Shore* house, but that first night back did go with a bang. The minute I saw Gary I was drawn to him like a magnet . . . but there was a twist. He'd gone and brought his mate Aaron with him, and Aaron was *A-mazing*! His whole upper body is covered in tattoos, like this human painting and he has twinkly eyes and a cheeky smile. I fancied Aaron from the minute he walked through the door, but I held back because no one knew about Gaz and me and it felt like there was unfinished business between us. Looking back, if there's one thing I would have done very differently it would have been the whole Gaz fling. Being with him was purely physical and when Aaron and I did eventually try to get together, Gary got in the way.

That night, though, we all piled into House of Smith in town and the minute we got back I couldn't wait to try out the waterbed, although the combination of Gary's monster cock and too many vodka cokes made me feel seasick. Of course, in the morning I had to pretend this was the first time I'd ever seen Gary's cock, even though I'd made very good friends with it a few months before.

When series eight finally aired, I think Mam was

shocked I was having sex on TV, but it sums *Geordie Shore* up: having fun; getting mortal and necking on with lads and lasses. What did upset me were the hundreds of Twitter trolls who branded me a slag. Why is it when a lad has sex on TV he's seen as a player but a lass gets ripped to shreds? Up until that point, I'd only ever had steady boyfriends and I'd never slept around. Anthony Hutton used to boast that when he was my boyfriend, I hadn't been with anyone else from Newcastle. Besides, I'd spent the whole of the last series more celibate than a nun!

For someone who claimed he wanted no-strings-attached sex, Gary changed his mind more often than he changed his bedsheets. One minute he said he didn't have any feelings for me, and the next he was jealous if I so much as spoke to another lad. In fact, Gary found it hard to even use the word 'feelings'. Like some alien life form, he didn't know what they were!

Then there was Scott to deal with. Thank God he was unaware that Gary and I had already slept together directly after series seven, because I reckon it would have kicked off there and then. That night Scott was clearly jealous of us getting close and he accused Gary of breaking lad code, but it's not like Scott and I ever had anything together. Scott made me so confused. 'If you're that bothered, maybe you and I should have gone there after all,' I thought. Sex with Gary was supposed to be a bit of harmless fun, but it was turning into a nightmare.

Then Gary accused me of telling Scott that, despite what was going on between him and me, I would always have feelings for Scott. The problem with being mortal is I never remember anything I've said, but even if I did say that to Scott, why the hell did Gary give a shit?

The atmosphere in the house changed again when Vicky re-entered the show and then Charlotte turned up. Of everyone, I was most nervous about Charlotte. Her and Gary's on–off relationship was over and she was totally loved up with her boyfriend, Mitch, who she described as her soulmate, but I didn't know how she was going to react. And, as Vicky said later in green screen: 'Marnie would flirt with a fucking lamp post.' That was one thing Vicky got right, although it was a bit like the pot calling the kettle black because it didn't take Vicky long before she was necking on with Aaron.

The worst part was that Charlotte arrived when me, Gary, Vicky and Aaron were in the middle of a candlelit dinner. Gary had just toasted his and my 'relationship' and then bloody Charlotte walks in. I thought my whole world was about to collapse! I prayed Charlotte would see me and Gary for what it was – a fling. Believe it or not, I wanted the girls to like me this time around. Thank God Charlotte didn't seem like she was going to lose sleep over it. But the me and Gary saga was causing all sorts of problems.

That house really does do mad things to you, because suddenly we'd find ourselves in way too deep! It all came to a head one night in Florita's when Scott started encouraging Aaron to flirt with me just to piss Gary off. To be fair, he didn't need much encouragement. After way too many tequilas, Aaron was completely mortal and he kept grabbing me and trying to kiss me. I put it down to Aaron being drunk – that's just what he's like – but Gary went mental and started giving me the third degree. *Please!*

'Do you know why I like Aaron more than you?' I shouted at him. 'Coz you've got no *fucking* heart!'

That really upset him. 'You just said Aaron was a nicer person than me; that he's got more feelings than me. OK, then. Go and shag Aaron!'

My emotions were all over the place because, the bottom line was, I *did* fancy Aaron but I'd been in denial about it since he'd come into the house. Aaron was a nicer person than Gary. I'd not noticed at first but the more we lived together the more my feelings for him developed. He wasn't obsessed with pulling girls in the same way Gary and Scott were, and that drew me towards him.

And I was starting to hate Gary. Gary is the sort of person who has this hard exterior and he goes out of his way to make girls think he doesn't care, when deep down he does. I thought, why can't you just be honest?

Although on screen it appeared like me and the girls were getting closer, the reality was very, very different. Charlotte and I did have a heart-to-heart about Gary, but I still didn't feel close to any of them. In fact, crazy as it sounds, I didn't feel like I fitted into *Geordie Shore* until at least series eleven.

But, as I said before, mad things happen and the weirdest had to be when Charlotte and I ended up kissing each other. *What the hell?* Neither of us can explain that one – I think we were just mortal. Also, I was so fed up with Gary saying he had feelings for me one minute and then telling me it was only sex the next. And, without Mitch, Charlotte was missing necking on with anyone. That said, I was quite happy to neck on with a girl, although Charlotte and I have *never* gone there since.

I didn't officially come out as bisexual until 2016, but in the run-up, I had realised I did find girls attractive. Nothing had ever *happened*, though. I remember when I was around eight kissing a girl called Amy at youth club. I used to practise my technique on her, which at that age was awful! She never said anything to me about it, but I think she was shocked. In my teens, I didn't actually do anything with girls either but there was definitely something going on because if I was ever on the sofa with my friends I'd always try to rub my feet in between their legs and against their vaginas. That's not normal, is it? Even now, though, I wouldn't say I was a lesbian. I'll always fancy boys and I've never had a full-on relationship with a girl. All I would say is that I'm open to girls and I don't categorise myself in any particular group. Why should I?

Mam doesn't get it at all. 'Marnie, man. What are you doing?' she always says, and it's hard to explain to her that I love kissing girls. In some ways, I love kissing girls more than I do boys. It's probably because there's not the same baggage. I can get the same attention from a girl that I can from a boy without half of the grief. Plus, it feels dead sexy and fun to kiss girls.

That night, I don't remember much about kissing Charlotte and I don't think tashing on with a lass is really Charlotte's thing, but it was light relief from all the house drama. Having said that, we did both wake up in the morning, look at each other, and think, *'What the fuck?'*

The relationship-that-never-should-have-been with Gary was beginning to come to a head, particularly after a trip to Manchester organised by Anna. We were due to host a singles night but it turned into the worst night out ever. Aaron and Holly ended up tearing strips out of each other because Aaron accused Charlotte of being this massive source of tension in the house. He'd claimed she'd caused a boy–girl divide. But Charlotte hadn't caused a divide! Gary had. Only days before, he'd organised a lads' night out to pie off all the girls. If there was anything that was going to cause tension, it was that. Gary couldn't get his head round the fact that him wanting to be the centre of the universe was tearing everyone apart.

For example, every time I went near Aaron, he'd kick off and accuse Aaron of breaking boy code; but Gary had done exactly the same to Scott! I kept thinking, 'How can you cock-block Aaron when five minutes after leaving series seven you were messaging me?' It didn't make sense. There was one rule for Gary and one rule for everyone else!

The whole situation was stressing me out so much. One minute I was telling Gary our relationship wasn't going to work out and we should just be friends, and the next I transformed into this green-eyed monster if I saw him necking on with other girls. What the fuck was wrong with me? One night at the Riverside I saw red. I don't think anyone had seen me have a pure radge moment before, and I shocked myself. It all kicked off when Gary started kissing this random right in front of me. That was it. I snapped and picked up the nearest object, which happened to be an ice bucket filled with water, and chucked it over them. I couldn't handle Gaz when he was mortal and I knew that if we didn't end things soon, we'd end up killing each other.

Salvation came in the form of newbie Kyle Christie. His arrival definitely took some heat out of the situation. Kyle was billed as my best mate from the outside, but that wasn't strictly true. I did know Kyle but not as well as the programme made out. And, at times, I'd found him attractive, but I hadn't banked on him being so annoying once he was inside the house. Kyle is a proper people-pleaser and he couldn't be himself on TV. I believe the only reason I've lasted in the show is because I am myself. I do stupid things. I upset people, and I'm not always proud of myself. But hopefully viewers can see I've got a kind side too.

Off camera, Kyle spent most of his time back-stabbing people – telling one person one thing and another something else so he could keep on-side with everyone. He'd swerve ever looking bad, and I'm sure that's why the producers got fed up with him. His routine got boring in the end.

Nevertheless, it was good to have him around at that moment because I was desperate to shake off Gary's evil spell and turn my attention to Aaron.

CHAPTER 11

SHIT HAPPENS. DRIVE ON.

Unbeknown to me, not long after Kyle arrived, he'd broken it to Aaron that I fancied him. At first when I found out, I was dead embarrassed but at the same time I had this urge to tell Aaron how I felt. Gary got in the way of everything, though. Why on earth did I ever get with him?

Unfortunately, I couldn't turn the clock back. I wanted to. So badly. One night, while Holly and Kyle were playing tonsil tennis on the dance floor in House of Smith, Aaron started necking on with a blonde lass Scotty T had already pulled at one the house parties. Not only was Scott furious but I was sooooooo jealous. 'Why can't that be me?' I thought. I tried so hard to hide how hurt I was, but I'm not great at covering my feelings at the best of times. The worst feeling was when Aaron brought her back to the house so he could get his end away in the shag pad. And I could have died when James and Kyle started mock-shagging on one of the chairs to take the piss out of Aaron losing his house virginity. Arrgghhhh!

Every time I got mortal and we went out together, all I wanted was to pull Aaron towards me and kiss him. I loved the way he looked at me, all doe-eyed. I could sense he fancied me, but something was holding him back. And that something was . . . *Gary*. Unsurprisingly, Gary was getting in the way of everything. Gary was ruining my life. Gary was putting himself at the centre of the fucking universe . . . again!

Even though Aaron admitted he wanted something to happen between us, he said it couldn't because he reckoned he'd be breaking 'boy code' with Gary. Apparently, they'd even talked about it and Aaron had told Gary he was going to be loyal to the lads. Hang on a minute! Gary didn't think twice about breaking boy code with Scott when he came round to my house and we had sex. For fear of upsetting Scott, I didn't want to tell the others how soon after series seven Gary had messaged me, but it was getting to the point where I was going to have to say something!

Then, Gary dropped another bombshell. He actually made me believe he'd had some sort of personality transplant. Instead of fanny-rat Gary beside me, I now had caring, sharing, sensitive Gary wanting to talk things through with me! On our way back from a night out in Leeds, he sat beside me in the minibus and poured his heart out. Great timing!

'Marnie, I was quite happy having a laugh, pulling you and going with you every night,' he said.

Was Gary trying to tell me he was happier going home with me than he was pulling other girls? What a load of shit!

'Then why did it start getting awkward when we stopped?' I asked him.

'Because you started telling Aaron you liked him. Don't try and mug me off with the Aaron thing,' he warned me.

As far as I could see, all Gary was doing was making sure me and Aaron didn't get together. But that night, I did catch a glimpse of a side to Gary I like. He was vulnerable and it told me he had feelings for me. The problem was Gary only revealed that part of himself on rare occasions and I needed him to be like that all the time. What Gary lacked, Aaron had. When I told the girls later how Gary had behaved and that I wished I could see more of his gentle side, Vicky couldn't wait to get a snide dig in.

'So. Just to confirm. It's Gary, not Aaron . . . ?' she called over sarcastically.

'Just to confirm; it's no one!'

And it was *still* no one by the time we went to Iceland with Tash-On Tours. Iceland was my first trip abroad with *Geordie Shore*, and I was so excited – not that I knew where Reykjavik actually was. Sadly, the reality of Iceland was far different. The minute we landed, I noticed how dark and miserable the city was – it was like being back in Stanley! I'm a girl who loves the sunshine, so I didn't get good vibes from Iceland at all. Take me to Ibiza! I kept thinking. Where's the sandy beach here? Nowhere! Emotionally, I was going through ups and downs, too. Not only was Vicky getting on my nerves, but the Aaron–Gary situation still wasn't sorted.

I was glad to get away from the others when Kyle, Holly, Aaron and I had a day trip out to the hot springs. But even that was awful. I'd looked at the guidebook Anna had given us beforehand and I'd seen an aqua blue lagoon with steam rising off the water. I had visions of this romantic backdrop with snow-capped mountains and me in my bikini seducing Aaron. Did we go to that place? No! There was no lagoon! We got taken to a shed beside a shitty pond in the middle of a bog. Even I couldn't look sexy in a pond! The water was warm, but that's where it ended. Apparently, this was supposed to be a naked spa, but I was not getting my fanny out for anyone, and Holly and I ended up paddling in our swimming cozzies and a T-shirt.

The only great thing about that day out was that me

and Aaron had some time to talk. Right in front of Kyle and Holly, he admitted he fancied me but he couldn't go there because of Gary. 'As much as we would like to, we can't,' he said. This was very frustrating. I couldn't help thinking that Aaron was being far too loyal to Gaz. He seemed to think Gaz would never trust him again. But I knew if the tables were turned, Gaz would fuck Aaron over in a heartbeat.

The producers had set up so many opportunities for Aaron and me to neck on, it was becoming a joke. In the end, I couldn't take it seriously. First, there'd been the hot spa and then they arranged for us to leave the club one night and enjoy the Northern Lights – just the two of us. Again, what should have been a romantic night under the Icelandic stars fell completely flat. There were no Northern Lights. It was pitch black and fucking freezing. I looked as bootylicious as a lollipop lady in my massive jacket and bobble hat, whereas I thought Aaron looked dead cute in his. Despite being alone and him telling me he wanted me, he *still* couldn't kiss me. I kept thinking, 'Aaron. Fuck lad code. I want your penis in my vagina!'

Again, it felt as if Gary had all the power, yet on this occasion he wasn't even there! Instead, we jumped back in the taxi and headed back to the club. I was going to have to be satisfied with knowing that in the future me and Aaron would happen. While my head was telling me this was totally fine, my fanny wasn't feeling as patient!

Back in Newcastle, shit was about to get real. I'd hated Iceland and I was glad to be home, but I'd decided on the plane that I wasn't going to let Gary control the situation anymore, whether Aaron liked it or not. Yes . . . it was time to drop the G-bomb! We'd been in Iceland for three days and we didn't have long until filming stopped. I had nothing to lose.

On one of our last nights out at Madame Koo's, I asked Aaron to kiss me, but he still wouldn't. Then I begged him . . . and he still wouldn't. I had on these gorgeous white hot-pants so I began grinding my arse on his lap. But he *still wouldn't go there*. No one could accuse me of not putting the graft in, but my God this was hard work. There was only one thing for it. I told Vicky that Gaz hadn't waited nearly as long before he and I had had sex as he'd made out to Aaron. The 'months' of waiting had been twenty-four hours! The one thing I could trust Vicky with was not keeping her trap shut. Prompted by a producer and a camera, she told the girls, the girls confronted Gaz and someone, who turned out to be James, later told Scotty T.

I did say later in green screen that I was glad the truth was out and that I didn't give a shit about Scott. Looking back, that was harsh. I did care about Scott's feelings. I just hated it more that Gary was the one obstacle keeping Aaron and me apart. To have it all out in the open was a relief. Yes, Scott was upset. And during the argument between him and Gaz, Gaz ended up smashing his fist through a window, getting in his car and driving off. Did I care? I thought he deserved everything that was being thrown at him and that Aaron finally needed to know what a complete dick Gary was.

And what Marnie wants, Marnie gets. On our last night of filming, Aaron came to see me upstairs. Everyone was mortal and chucking each other in the hot tub, but me and Aaron were spooning and kissing in the girls' bedroom. I was buzzing! I'd got the lad I was after all along, but even then we didn't have sex. It was enough just to be close to each other.

Given the endless toing and froing that had gone on between us, I didn't think twice about reaching out to him once filming was over. But despite a few texts between us, he made it obvious he didn't want to know. *What the hell?* I found that impossible to understand. How come one minute he was like a dog with a bone and now, when the cameras weren't rolling, he'd gone off the boil? I was later to discover that all the time Aaron had been in the house, he'd had a girlfriend on the outside called Becca. When I think about it, I suspect the phone calls he used to make were to her. We're only allowed one phone call a week from the red phone box in the house and in the early days I always called Mam. We'd have these intense, emotional conversations, because some drama or another would always be kicking off. Aaron would also be talking on the phone for ages but none of us ever clocked that he was in a relationship.

At the time, I was also having stresses finding a good agent. This is an element of being on TV that I had no clue about whatsoever. Whereas the housemates usually help each other out with recommending good people, they didn't with me. I'm convinced it's because, at first, they didn't want me to be successful. Anyway, I hadn't gelled well with my initial management. They never paid me on time and work outside of the show wasn't picking up either.

Having earned some money, I eventually passed my driving test. But, let me tell you, Marnie with wheels was a bloody miracle! The theory test alone took me seven attempts. Yes ... seven! Whereas previously I'd have to stop because I couldn't afford to resit the test, now, every time I failed I just put in for another one immediately. I was so determined!

As for the practical, I'd already failed it twice but I hadn't given up hope. Nana was a true inspiration on that score. I kept remembering how she used to pick me up from school and I thought, 'If she can do it, so can I!' The day of my test being my birthday may have helped, too. 'I'm twenty-two today so you'd better be nice to me,' I told the examiner the minute I got into the car, hoping he'd take pity on me. The problem was I'd never *actually* had a lesson. When I was with Mark all those years before, he had taught me how to drive, but I'd always got so nervous in the tests that I was handed a big fat *Fail* at the end of every single one of them. Then he'd bought me that car so I could eventually use it when I passed but then sold it without me ever driving it as I couldn't bear the thought that he bought me something to keep me sweet. To hear the words, 'Marnie, well done, you've passed!' was unbelievable.

Mam and Eric came with me that day and the examiner even let me drive us all home. From then on, I drove Mam *everywhere*. It was so liberating for us both. Even if she wanted to go five minutes down the road, she got a lift in my new Citroen DS3, which I loved because it was glossy white and ultra-sporty. Over the years, Mam had struggled so much with getting from A to B, always having to rely on someone else to take her places, so I was made up I could do that for her – especially as I'd convinced myself I'd never be able to drive or own my own car. Driving also meant I could travel further afield and I started enjoying the odd night out in Manchester and even drove down to London a few times with mates.

Around this time, Sophie and I started to reconnect, which I was so relieved about. Her silence had been awful. 'We're family. And family stick together,' I kept saying to Mam, although I did understand why Sophie had been so off with me. The funny thing was that the whole time Sophie was in *Geordie Shore* she kept threatening to leave and saying she was never going to go back for another series. Yet when she got booted out, it was completely the opposite. She was devastated! And because she'd made it clear that she didn't want to speak to me, I'd got on with my life. But I did miss her.

'Fancy meeting up and going out, there's a party in town . . .' she wrote to me.

'I'd love to!'

I didn't hesitate, and although Sophie and I didn't sit down and thrash out what had happened, it was brilliant that we could go out again without bringing the whole *Geordie Shore* epic up. My mam had even stopped talking to Sophie's mam after it all kicked off – it was that much of a drama! Sophie and I becoming mates again was a gradual reconnection, but it was a reconnection that was well overdue.

CHAPTER 12

YOUR MARIGOLDS ARE CALLING

It would be the understatement of the century to say that Vicky Pattison and I did not get on. By series nine I couldn't stand the girl and I couldn't understand why the others seemed to like her so much. Vicky was older than all of us, but I didn't think that gave her the right to boss people around in the house the way she did. I forgot to mention that at the end of the last series her and Gary necked on, which was the most hilarious turn up for the books. As far as I was concerned, they were perfect for each other. They both wanted to be the centre of attention and as much as Vicky accused me of running the 'Marnie Show', she did exactly the same, only I called it the 'Vicky Pattison Experience'. But I can say this much: my experience of Vicky was driving me to distraction and I could feel it was going to kick off sooner or later.

I was also starting to hate my time in the house and I wondered how long I'd be able to keep going back.

'I'm proud of you whatever you want to do,' Mam told me during one of our many conversations.

'Yeah, but Mam, *Geordie Shore*'s all I've got. I don't know what else I *can* do! And I've never been a quitter.'

'Just go in there and be yourself like you've always done. The producers love you.'

I could always rely on Mam to support me. And I figured me and the girls had got a bit closer, in particular Charlotte. She and I had some good girlie chats and she was the person I would automatically go to if I wanted to discuss something serious. I still hadn't truly bonded with Holly, even though it's funny to think that she's now one of my best friends.

With hindsight, I think Charlotte and I would have bonded more had it not been for her boyfriend, Mitch. She was deeply in love with him and spent a lot of time miserable because she couldn't be with him and she'd leave at the drop of a hat to see him – sometimes in the middle of a night out! She'd even made a mould of her shaven fairy to send him as a keepsake, only it came out a weird colour and lopsided.

As far as Charlotte was concerned he was *The One*. We'd only met Mitch once when we'd gone clubbing in London with the show, but he was so pissed when he turned up that I don't recall speaking to him. All I remember was him saying, 'Hi' to Gary then falling all over Charlotte, yanking her hair and trying to dry hump her on the sofa. Then he called her the C-word and made her cry. We all thought, 'My God! This is the love of Charlotte's life and he's calling her the C-word!' It's hardly the most romantic line on the planet, is it?

As soon as filming started it was obvious something was not right between them. I felt sad for Charlotte. She'd been going out with Mitch for what seemed like ages and she genuinely thought they were going to be together forever. Having a relationship on the outside is really tough when you are in the show. First of all, there's the demon drink to deal with and getting mortal and keeping your knickers on is *really* hard. Then, if you're a flirt like me, there's the hassle of convincing a boyfriend that it is just flirting and *nothing* happened. We're in the house to have fun and stir shit up but sometimes innocent moves can get blown out of all proportion. It took me a long time to realise that our lives in the show aren't normal. It's TV and we play up to the cameras but when we leave our lives aren't normal either. I was to learn that down the line with my serious boyfriends Ricky Rayment and Lewis Bloor. Starring in a reality programme like *Geordie Shore* can put a lot of pressure on a relationship.

As for me and Aaron, can you believe that was still dragging on? When I think about it now, it's not even funny how tedious it became. It was almost as epic as *Titanic* without Aaron ever getting to the point where he declared his undying love for me! Having said that, he looked totally amazing when he turned up with a black T-shirt on and slicked-back hair. I hadn't seen him during the break at all, and I didn't know whether I'd still be attracted to him. Two seconds through the door, though, and I fancied him so much it hurt. And from our first night out it was obvious the spark was still there. Believe me, it would have been easier if it wasn't! We carried on like we'd never been away.

I had done some thinking, though. I'd decided I wanted a relationship with Aaron, not just a fling. I wasn't going to let my knickers drop at the first sight of him. Playing hard to get was almost impossible because all I wanted to do was rip his clothes off and shag him. But, as we'd only ever kissed, I didn't want to mess with that Feng Shui.

On our first night out we were flirting ridiculously. And I mean *ridiculously*.

'You look nice tonight,' he said.

That was an ego boost, and I found myself replying, 'You know I've got a massive soft spot for you.' Playing it cool wasn't going as well as I'd hoped, but we did agree that we still fancied each other and we'd see what happened.

That night Aaron was mortal and he kept grabbing

me and hugging me when we got back to the house. I didn't know what the state of play was with his girlfriend Becca but I did think it was strange that he was so full-on now, because he hadn't been when I'd texted him outside of *Geordie Shore*. Now, he even tried to get in my bed and take his boxers off!

'I don't care what you do, Aaron, as long as you don't try to cop a feel,' I said. Within minutes of him hopping in with me he was fast asleep. Phew!

I genuinely thought Aaron would have much more respect for me if I waited. Plus, I'd sort of hooked up with a guy called Dan Slone during our break and I wasn't sure how things were going to go with him. He wasn't my boyfriend or anything – I'd been to a house party in Newcastle and we'd had a drunken kiss so it was all very casual. I'd actually known Dan for ages from being out clubbing. I'd always thought he was fit, but never saw him in 'that way'. He had blonde hair and cheeky eyes and he was so down to earth. One of the qualities I really liked about Dan was that he was so laid back – not a stresshead at all. Like me, he wasn't from Newcastle, but he'd grown up just north of the city in Morpeth. It wasn't until we kissed that I thought, 'Mmmm. Maybe you are more attractive than I'd given you credit for in the past.' I did start to feel differently about him.

When it comes to *Geordie Shore,* I know others like Aaron went in there pretending they were single just so they could neck on, but I've never been like that. If I have a boyfriend I am always straight up about it, and if I make mistakes while I'm in there, then I'll take the rap. See what I mean when I say I'm 100 per cent myself when I enter the house? Others aren't so honest, even the girls, but I don't believe in lying.

Because Dan wasn't serious, though, I didn't make a big deal of him. In fact, he was to become my full-on boyfriend later down the line, and I told everyone in the house when that happened. Whatever I am, I'm truthful!

Anyway, Aaron can't have been that serious about me because after I refused to shag him, he seemed to think this was a one-way ticket to fanny heaven – just not mine! Only hours after calling me his 'girlfriend' in front of the whole house, he was in the club trying to get a girl's number. I knew he was joking when he called me his girlfriend, but I couldn't help getting butterflies. This sudden change in behaviour was baffling.

The worst thing about him getting a girl's number was that Aaron was doing it right in front of my nose! But karma came to my rescue ... the girl who he'd been grafting all night was now in the middle of the dance floor necking on with Scotty T. I felt so hurt by Aaron because he'd lied to us, but I was secretly happy when it all kicked off again between him and Scott. Aaron looked like a prick! Scott claimed he didn't know Aaron was trying to pull the same lass.

Whatever the truth, arguing in front of me about it was mortifying. Aaron was so desperate to neck on with this lass and I couldn't help thinking, '*What the hell?* Didn't we have something going on? Why are you arguing over a complete random?' That night Aaron acted like such a dick, and he went right down in my estimation. I thought, 'There's no way you're going to walk all over me like that.' So Marnie did the sensible thing and got a taxi home. Er, no . . . I wish! No, Marnie did the sensible thing and swilled Aaron. Yes, I threw my drink all over him. Oh my God! I actually did that! Only moments before I could feel the anger welling up inside me and I snapped. It wasn't my finest moment, but I don't regret it.

I do regret what happened next, though. Instead of staying away from Aaron, like I should have done, I forgave him . . . again. And we necked on in the club . . . again. And we spooned in bed . . . again. What was wrong with me? However much I tried I couldn't shake the Aaron spell. But Aaron had this habit of building me up and knocking me down.

Exactly the same happened when we had a house party for Holly's birthday. Aaron and I were getting on so well until the girl whose number he'd been trying to get in the club walked in. *What the fuck?* I reckoned if Aaron didn't want to go there with her, then he wouldn't have invited her. And, sure enough, as the night went on and I got more mortal, they got closer and closer. What I didn't know was that it was Gaz who'd encouraged Aaron to ring her, just to get back at me. That was such a low move!

The disappointing thing was, I'd made a real effort to look nice for Aaron. I'd spent ages getting my fake tan even and I had on a black leotard with black feathers and sexy knee-high boots. I wanted him to want me so badly, but the minute this girl rocked up, I knew she was out of my league. She was super slim with a sexy white dress on and scraped-back hair. I could not compete! I don't remember too much about what happened next but the girls kindly filled me in the next morning. I've never been able to watch that episode back because I lost it so badly. Not only was I writhing around the floor with my arse hanging out in front of Aaron, but I had a mega meltdown outside and Kyle had to run out to calm me down.

Aaron acting like that made me want to get back at him so badly. So I did. The minute I got back in the house, I pulled Kyle towards me and snogged the face off him. Kyle? Whooaaa! I'd never even fancied Kyle! He was a mate. I cannot explain that one at all. Later, he said in green screen it was like kissing his sister. Steady on, Kyle! I don't think I'm that bad!

That night, I know I ruined Holly's birthday party. It was supposed to be special and Vicky and Charlotte had arranged for the whole house to be decked out like an enchanted forest. By the time I jumped into a cab to see Mam, it had turned into a dark fairy tale. I had the biggest ups and downs in that series and, at times, it felt like I was losing my mind.

What was really annoying was that I didn't go to Paris, either. I learned later the next day that Anna had rung and told the whole crew they had a job out there. I would have loved to have joined them, but it was better for everyone that I left to get my head together.

In total I left the house for four days. First off, I went to see Mam. She'd got so used to me needing a break when everything kicked off in the house. I didn't go out either, other than to see Dan. It was proper chill-out time.

Surprisingly, by the time I did re-enter the house, people said they had missed me, but inside I still felt very fragile. I was genuinely sorry for kissing Kyle and using him to get back at Aaron, and one of the first things I did was put my hands up and admit I'd been wrong. The last thing I wanted was for him to be given the cold shoulder over a situation I'd created. The boys had even started calling me Mad Dog Marnie! I was so embarrassed.

One of the nicer developments was that Aaron and I also had a heart-to-heart. And we both apologised to each other. Even so, the whole atmosphere was on a knife edge. An argument could kick off at any time. As it turned out, it didn't take long. While Aaron was on one side messing with my head, Vicky was on the other. As far as I was concerned, they could both do one.

Vicky had been asked by Anna to be 'team leader', which meant that on all the nights out we had to work for Tash-On Tours, Vicky was running the show. To top it all, she'd turned up at the beginning of the series with her hair dyed blonde. She looked like a cross between a poor man's Marilyn Monroe and Margaret Thatcher! She was so full of herself now that she was in charge. Being around Vicky made me feel like I was back at Brinkburn High School with a load of shitty teachers telling us what to do. She did my head in. Plus, she was on this mission to grass me up with Anna, which made me realise how much she had it in for me.

In one task the whole house had to make 200 origami birds for a Japanese party Anna was holding. I wasn't going to sit there and work for Vicky. Besides, I couldn't even pronounce the word origami, let alone do it! I'm like me mam when it comes to understanding instructions. I'm a total stresshead. I panic and freak out. Simple as. Despite all the others not pulling their weight (we only managed to fold 100 in the end), Vicky was so desperate to look like she'd been doing her job that she singled me out as the person who'd worked the least.

'Marnie's spent most of her time up in bed. She

couldn't be arsed,' I heard her whinge on to Anna. Then she accused me of 'making the energy go down in the group'. Oh My God! Was she having a laugh? I thought, 'Who the fuck does she think she is?'

Not only that, but she went on to claim that I didn't put any effort in on one work night out, which was total bullshit. One of my tasks was to place as many kisses on Scotty T's naked torso as I could. As Aaron was looking on, I was more than happy to go the extra mile to make him jealous. Scott had so many bright red lipstick marks over him, he looked like he'd caught measles. I couldn't have worked faster, yet the following evening she accused me of not pulling my weight and she demanded I do the dishes before hitting the club. 'Marnie, your Marigolds are calling,' that boss bitch said to me. 'Fuck right off, Vicky,' I thought. 'Why should I clean up everybody's dirty dishes?' No, Marnie had had enough. Marnie was going to stand her ground and do precisely nothing. But the minute Vicky realised I hadn't lifted a finger, she came at me with another punishment. Now, I wasn't allowed out until I'd cleaned the whole kitchen. Outwardly, I was playing it cool so as not to give Vicky the satisfaction, but I was spitting underneath.

Unfortunately, Vicky had such a strong personality, she could turn everyone in the house against you with the click of her fingers. She was singling me out and alienating me from the whole group. Vicky had that power, but I needed her to know she couldn't speak to me like that.

One of the biggest stresses about living in the *Geordie Shore* house is that every tiny argument can turn into a major explosion. As I've said, there's something about being in there that makes everyone go a bit cuckoo. Nevertheless, I'm stubborn. I waited until everyone left the house, shoved enough dishes in the dishwasher for the house to eat off, then piled the rest in a black bin liner and wedged it underneath a seat so it looked like I'd cleaned up. I couldn't stop giggling all the time I was doing it. It was time to get some slap on and join the others.

Needless to say, the next morning when Vicky discovered what I'd done, she was foaming and she emptied all the dirty dishes out on my bed. So by the time she announced she'd had enough and wasn't coming back after the end of the series, I was glad to see the back of her. The others couldn't stop bawling when she broke the news at our Christmas meal. There was this big emotional build-up before she blurted it out, but I think the others were only upset because Vicky had been an original cast member. Off camera, I don't reckon they were that bothered. I tried to hide it, but no one understood how happy I was.

CHAPTER 13

PLASTIC FANTASTIC?

People always ask me if TV has changed my life for the better. I always say yes, but if there's one thing I could change, it's how I started to feel about my appearance. Seeing myself made me very insecure, as did all the trolls on Twitter. As I mentioned, the main focus was my nose. All these people saying that it was huge was gutting. I'd never even had a problem with my nose before, but now I fixated on it. Every time I looked in the mirror, I felt so self-conscious.

'Just ignore it, pet. You're gorgeous,' Mam would say to me. But I couldn't. It wasn't even as if I was getting papped by any photographers at that point, which is a whole different level of pressure, but it was enough for me to want to make changes.

Aside from my nose, one part of my body I'd never been comfortable with was my boobs. So not long after we finished filming, I booked myself in for an uplift. Not being experienced at cosmetic surgery, I took advice from the others in the house. Admittedly, I didn't do any proper research myself. I now deeply regret that. If there's one piece of advice I'd give to anyone wanting a nose job or a boob job or even just getting lip fillers, is to find out exactly what the procedure is and the reputation of the person doing it. I did neither.

The problem with my boobs was that I hated the shape of them. Ever since I'd developed they'd not been symmetrical and I hated how big and low my nipples were. If I hadn't been on TV, I guess I would have lived with my imperfections, but being on screen highlights all your physical flaws – a bit like a huge imaginary red arrow above each one constantly pointing at them.

As well as all the attention I was getting on social media, I've always been very hard on myself, too, so I think that also prompted my decision. I couldn't stop pulling myself apart. All of a sudden, I was trawling through Instagram looking at celebrities and picking out all the features from different people that I liked. I thought, 'I'll have lips like Katie Price and boobs like Heidi Montag off *The Hills* and hair like Kim Kardashian.' Now, I've realised it's wrong to want to be someone else. You should only want to be the best version of yourself.

I'm convinced the Aaron situation also had an impact. As daft as it sounds, the way Aaron had behaved by necking on with me one minute and mugging me off the next had made me feel so low. Whenever he tried to pull other girls I thought, 'Why am I not good enough? What do I have to do to be attractive?' Crazy, huh? Had I not fancied Aaron so much maybe I wouldn't have been that bothered but, unlike my fling with Gary, I *really* liked him and I genuinely thought we could be together.

Most girls who have breast surgery want bigger boobs, but I didn't want bigger boobs at all. I wanted *my* boobs, but just a perkier, pointier version of them. I'd always been a C cup and I've remained one. A 34C to be precise. What I envisioned was their shape changing. For that reason, I didn't opt for implants. I wanted a breast uplift, which is a different procedure.

When I first went to see the surgeon, he explained what would happen like this: 'It's like cutting out a triangular segment from a pie. Once the skin is removed, the pie is then pulled in tighter and stitched together so each boob is lifted up. Then the nipples are removed and positioned higher.'

It sounded very straightforward, but perhaps I should have listened to my gut instinct. I don't want to reveal the name of the surgeon because I did end up getting my money back, but he was so grumpy when I had my first consultation. I didn't warm to him at all. And he didn't explain to me all the downsides to the operation either. Believe me, I've had so many problems and I'll have to live with his mistakes for the rest of my life.

Even though my surgery cost me £5,000, I was so caught up with what my new boobs would look like and how much happier I'd be, that those doubts went straight to the back of my mind. Marnie in denial . . . again! I wasn't that bothered about going under either. Needles or operations aren't something I get nervous about – although I didn't enjoy the feeling of being put to sleep. Some girls I know love it when the anaesthetic kicks in, but not me. Instead, all I kept thinking about was when I could see the finished results.

In my head, I was going to have the *best boobs ever*. But this is the mistake lots of people make when they have plastic surgery. Exactly like me, they imagine the end result being the image that they've dreamed about. Spoiler alert – it doesn't happen! I don't want to burst any bubbles here but, for that reason, I think plastic surgery can be very disheartening because no one ever truly gets the results they want. Perhaps that's why girls become addicted to it? We're always seeking perfection and I've learned there is no such thing.

That's my experience, anyway. I'm sure if you asked the same question to others from *Geordie Shore* you'd get a different answer. Charlotte, for example, was over the moon with the nose job she had last year. While she moaned about it being painful, she adored her new look. Disappointingly, I was not so enthusiastic about mine!

Despite feeling so groggy the minute I got out of theatre, I was excited to rip off my dressings to see the results. Frustratingly, I had to wait. The pain didn't hit me straight away either, because I was so dosed up on painkillers after the op. When it did, it was agonising. I had these stabbing pains in my chest that shot through my whole body. And I couldn't shower for days. That was so mingin'. Me mam said I smelled like a tin of rancid tuna. I'd not anticipated how low I'd feel, but I was about to get even lower.

Sadly, the results were not even close to what I'd wanted. I loved the pert, round shape the surgeon had created, but when I returned to the clinic to have the dressings removed, the scarring was horrendous. No joke, it was like a wild animal had attacked me! I couldn't hide my disappointment. When I lifted up each boob all I could see were these luminous pink jagged knife marks, like I was the victim in some crime drama. Those scars didn't just run underneath each boob, either. The surgeon makes what's called an anchor scar, so one incision runs from underneath the breast right up to the nipple. Whereas I could hide the other scars, those were so, so obvious.

'How long will the scarring be like that?'

'Oh, it will heal after a few months.'

'Thank God for that!'

But the scarring didn't heal and my nipples weren't the same size either. One was noticeably larger than the other. I looked like a freak! In fact, a year later I had to have corrective surgery on both my boobs and a botched nose job. And while the scars around my boobs now look 100 per cent better than they did, I'll probably be scarred for life.

Directly after the op there was the swelling and bruising to get used to. I'd never had a bruised boob before – was it even possible? I thought, 'Could my life get any worse?' Yes! When my left boob got infected I nearly died. Thank God I had Mam and Eric and friends like Lowis around for moral support. At one point there was a gaping hole in the scar. And I've not even got to the pus yet. If you're eating while reading this, well done for multi-tasking, but it's probably the right moment to stop. My boobs oozed green pus and wept other indescribable fluids for months. Sorry!

Then I developed all these lumps around my nipples where little scars had formed. At times it looked like I had wire popping out from my boobs. I became very self-conscious because if I wore any clothing with thin material, it showed. Of course, when I got back to *Geordie Shore*, Gary Beadle always made comments about my boobs. 'What's wrong with your nipples?' he kept asking. Typical, sensitive Gary!

I was so unhappy, and I was desperate for *something* to go right. And that's what I mean. Once you start having plastic surgery, it's hard not to start looking at every part of yourself and picking holes in what you see. I'm not saying that's a good thing, it's just how it is.

Not long afterwards I booked myself in for the nose job with a surgeon who had been recommended to me by Aaron. This time around, I did a little more checking up about the clinic. But again, I wish, wish, wish, I'd done some proper research. For another £5,000 procedure, it couldn't have been worse. I wanted the perfect nose, like the Disney princess nose on all the cartoons: thin, petite and slightly curved – like a miniature ski jump. It's impossible to see what you've got until the swelling goes down but I knew something was wrong soon after.

Again, I wasn't that bothered about having an operation, although I couldn't have predicted how painful it was to have the plugs removed the next day. Nose plugs are like having two massive tampons up each nostril. And the night of my operation was horrendous. Having to breathe out of my mouth for twenty-four hours made me sound like an overweight walrus. When I returned for the surgeon to take them out . . . Owwwwwwww! It felt like he was going to drag my brain through each nostril. To reshape my nose, they'd broken the bones with a hammer and so I also had to wear a splint for a whole week. If you think about this procedure too much, it makes you want to vomit, so I try not to dwell on it.

After my splint had been removed I'd been warned the swelling would continue till it reached its peak. The surgeon wasn't wrong. Seven days after my op, my face looked like a fully inflated beach ball. I couldn't stop looking at it and touching it and I noticed an ultra hard little bump.

'Can you feel this bump?' I asked Mam, making her run her fingers over it.

'Marnie, man. Will you stop going on about the bump! It's the swelling!'

She was so frustrated with me, as were all my mates. 'It's in your head,' they kept saying. Or, they said, 'If you're always going to be this unhappy, you shouldn't get surgery done.'

I messaged my surgeon to tell him, but he said that whatever it was it would go down with the swelling. But it didn't. It got worse. It wasn't a bump. It transformed into a full-on spike sticking out of my face like a devil's horn. Apparently, it was a callous, which is quite rare. Only one in five people get them after a nose job. Surprise, surprise, it had to be me, didn't it? The actual spike is cartilage that's grown over the bone.

The problem is you can't have another nose job for a full year until the first one has completely healed, so I'd have to wait twelve months before anything could be done about it. I was fuming. I had the most awful boobs on the planet and now I had a spike on my nose. My friends called it 'the spike' too, which made me want to die. And then everyone in the *Geordie Shore* house did the same. Bring on the depression session!

When I eventually had the procedures fixed, I spent ages looking for the perfect surgeon to do the job – exactly what I should have done first time around. At last I struck lucky with my miracle worker Dr Hasan who is based in Birmingham. If ever there was a saviour of crimes against surgery it's him – like my cosmetic guardian angel!

To sort my boobs out he had to carry out something called scar revision, which basically means he had to make a whole new set of scars to cover the old ones. Crazy, huh? Don't ask me how that works, either, because I've never been able to figure it out. Anyway, it was a risky procedure because I could have ended up with even worse scarring, but thankfully I didn't. My boobs will never be scar-free but he's done an amazing job. I can now take my clothes off in front of someone without automatically wanting to hide them with both hands!

As for my nose, Dr Hasan said he wouldn't be able to shave down the callous fully without shattering the bone again. The thought of spending another year with a hideous swelling did not appeal, so he's done the best he can. I notice the bump when I run my fingers along it, but it's not sticking out of my face anywhere near as much as it was before. And I've had a bit of filler put in on the other side so it's not so noticeable. See what I mean? Once you start tinkering it's hard to stop.

I do feel more confident now, but another procedure that I went too heavy on was lip filler. I wish I could go back to the beginning and have my lips done all over again. At first, I had a tiny bit of filler put in. Many of you reading this won't have ever had filler, so let me explain: the actual lip filler is an acid that our bodies naturally produce, only it's injected into you and makes your lips plump up. Surprise, surprise, I overdid it. My lips are only small, but after the first treatment, I wanted more; and after the second I wanted my lips injected again. The more I kept going, the bigger they got. By the end, my lips were so plumped up that I was starting to get trout pout. I could see it, but I still wanted more. Weird, eh?

The treatment is not permanent. But if I haven't had filler for a while, I can tell my lips haven't gone back to their natural shape. The bottom line is I should only have had my lips enhanced, instead of altering them completely. And whatever people say about the treatment not being painful, they are lying. The injection itself doesn't hurt, but the swelling takes a day or so to go down and my lips always ache like mad. My worry is I've stretched the skin so much that if the filler wasn't there, they'd be wrinkly or collapse.

I think I'm what's called a cosmetic surgery car crash. I even appeared on *Celebrity Botched Up Bodies* at the beginning of this year to talk about my ordeal at the hands of bad surgeons. I described how it had affected my self-esteem and how I constantly worry about how I look. I suppose I want to warn girls who are thinking about plastic surgery to research properly and make sure it's really what you want. And always find the best qualified surgeon that you can afford.

While I got loads of messages of support, I also started to get a lot of wisecracks about my *Geordie Shore* intro, too. Obviously, after my plastic surgery, I remained at the start of the programme saying, 'I'm Marnie. I'm twenty. I'm a natural beauty. Real boobs. Real hair and a really good arse.' But did trolls think I was stupid? I know I don't have real boobs now, nor am I 100 per cent a natural beauty, but when the VT was recorded, I was. The opening intros for the show are down to the programme and if trolls want to have a pop, they should contact the show's producers. *That* got very boring!

The results of my boob job and my nose job were

out of my control. My filler and disastrous liposuction, on the other hand, was completely down to me.

Hands up – with the liposuction I didn't follow the rules like I was supposed to, so I've only got myself to blame. I'd wanted liposuction on my stomach because I'd porked out a bit. When you're in *Geordie Shore* you do eat a lot of crap takeaways, kebabs and pizzas late at night and then there's all the booze. At one point, I'd ballooned up to my heaviest weight of 9st 10lb and I got so much abuse on social media that I went on this massive health kick and cut out dairy and red meat. As well as training hard, my diet was really low fat. I lost 17lb! This time around, though, I wanted to lose weight super quick so I opted for surgery.

The problem was that after the operation, I was supposed to wear this horrible elasticated body suit for six days, but I didn't. Instead, I went out and got mortal. It meant my stomach started to develop ripples in it, and for some unknown reason it went all discoloured, too. The ripples and the weird yellowish colour are gradually getting better with the help of some heavy-duty massage, but the worst part is the holes that have been left where the surgeon inserts tubes called cannula – these are used to suck out all the fat. I have two holes in the small of my back which you can barely notice, but the other two are like boreholes on either side of my pubic bone, directly above my vagina. Every time I look at them I feel totally gutted. You can't miss them – it's like someone's been drilling for oil next to my fairy. I still don't know whether those holes will ever disappear. My vagina is the one part of my body that I've always been dead proud of. I've always reckoned it was lovely.

CHAPTER 14

THE ALIEN HAS LANDED!

I never thought there'd be a time when something or someone otherworldly would enter *Geordie Shore* until I met Chloe Ferry. Believe me, I'm the first person to swear I've seen a ghost or a UFO, or to say I've got a connection to the spirit world. In fact, if you don't believe in vampires, werewolves, unicorns, fairies and mermaids then I don't want to know. But, until I'd met Chloe, I'd never claimed to have met an alien.

Don't get me wrong, I loved Chloe from day one. In fact, she saved me in that house. Just when I thought I might not be able to last another series, in she walked with another newbie, Nathan Henry. But Chloe is the daftest, funniest person I think I've ever met. She even looks like an alien! And she talks so fast that half of the time I have no idea what she's saying! She's one of a kind.

This time around James had decided he'd had enough and, after episode two, he didn't return to the show. Talk about destabilising the house! Although James was boring in that he didn't neck on with lasses, or have fights, or spew everywhere, he was calm, and great when you needed someone level-headed to inject some sanity into the conversation. It's weird how one person leaving or arriving in *Geordie Shore* can change the dynamic of the house completely. I suppose that's how the housemates felt when I arrived and now I was seeing it first-hand. If the previous episodes of *Geordie Shore* were mental, series ten felt like a white-knuckle rollercoaster ride – and we only filmed for four and a half weeks! Thank God I found a friend in Chloe.

Whereas Aaron and I had been the never-quite-happened romance of the show, Charlotte and Gaz was the most on–off relationship ever. As I've said before, when Charlotte was with Mitch, she didn't care where Gary stuck his willy. She'd even given her blessing to my fling with him. But now Charlotte and Mitch had split up, all bets were off.

The Charlotte–Mitch break-up was painful because she'd been head over heels for him, but it hadn't been working out for some time. They argued a lot and inside the house Charlotte was so miserable. Much of the problem was that Mitch didn't want Charlotte to be in *Geordie Shore*, and it created tension. As I've said before, I didn't understand that properly until I later went out with Ricky Rayment from *TOWIE*. Boyfriends on the outside feel so threatened when you're inside the house. Guys can be territorial like that.

Charlotte had been in no man's land with Mitch for so long that when they finally finished in series nine, she needed a shoulder to cry on. It just so happened that shoulder was . . . Gary! They'd not kissed or had sex with each other for two years! Charlotte had sworn that when she'd got Gary out of her system the last time around she'd never go there again, but I swear Gaz has superpowers that automatically draw girls to his cock!

So, when Chloe and Nathan arrived, I still fancied Aaron even though we'd still *never shagged*! Besides, during the break I'd been seeing more and more of Dan Slone. I thought if I waited any longer for Aaron my vagina might close up. Being in a house with Aaron was worse than being in a desert without an oasis. Dan was fun, though. And despite what he thought, I didn't count him as serious – more of a whirlwind romance – but I did go into series ten telling everyone I had a boyfriend. Like I said, I'm not the sort of person to cheat and if I'm with someone, I'm with someone. If I fuck up I'm on camera, it's not like I can hide from my mistakes!

But Charlotte? Charlotte wasn't even in a proper relationship with Gary but suddenly she'd turned into this rabid hyena if anyone so much as spoke to him. That fucked me off big style, because I *always* talked to Gary. I even flirted with him, but by then there was nothing between me and Gary. *Nothing.*

Charlotte got the wrong end of the stick from the very start. To begin with, on our first night out with the newbies, Charlotte had to be removed from the club by security because she attacked me. All I'd been doing was dancing with Gaz and she went proper berserk. Then Holly piled in and started belittling me so I ended up swilling her. Nightmare! I didn't deserve the way Charlotte treated me and Holly probably didn't deserve to have my drink thrown over her. I was fuming, though.

What made me sad was that for such a long time it'd been so hard being in the house, but it had felt like we'd turned a corner. Charlotte and I had been getting closer. Even though Holly and Kyle were almost in a full-on relationship, I'd been spending quality time with Holly too. In a heartbeat, it felt like we were back to square one. And I felt dead sorry for Chloe and Nathan. It was their first night in the house and it had been totally fucked up!

Thank God Charlotte did the decent thing and apologised to me the next day. I actually did feel sorry for her because it was clear that the whole Gary situation was messing with her head. She looked genuinely upset and that got even worse after she had a heart-to-heart with Gary.

None of us thought Gaz was capable of being in a proper relationship with anyone, but apparently he was. Whaaaaaat? Gary Beadle has feelings for someone? Call the love police! He confessed to Charlotte that he'd met a girl called Lillie over the break and he wanted to give it a go. None of us saw that one coming! I felt gutted for Charlotte. Over the years she'd put so much energy into trying to make Gaz fall in love with her and there he was with someone else. He was even phoning this girl and *missing* her, and talking about her like she was his proper girlfriend.

Charlotte had lost loads of weight, too. And she looked amazing. I don't know exactly how much she lost but it must have been around three or four stone. As well as doing *Geordie Shore*, she'd been doing a fitness DVD where she had to pile on the pounds, then sweat it all off and stay away from Chinese takeaways. She'd breezed in looking dead confident only to be knocked down by Gary . . . again!

Meanwhile, I was enjoying having two people around that I really liked. As I said, Chloe is just crazy. For a girl who'd almost been a champion ice skater before *Geordie Shore*, she couldn't have been more clumsy. When we went to an ice rink the day after the bust-up she was this graceful swan gliding around and pirouetting like a ballerina. But on the dance floor? She was a truly awful dancer.

Chloe can be surprising and so stupid at the same time. For example, there was a period when all the girls in the house were obsessed with wearing coloured contact lenses. We had loads of them because we loved how they made our eyes look really sparkly. One night, Chloe was so palatic that before she slept she took hers out and put them in her glass of water next to the bed. But she drank them! She *actually* drank them. She woke up thirsty in the night and necked the whole glass – contact lenses, the lot. And she chewed the veneers off her teeth! I've only had my teeth whitened, but she had these temporary veneers on while she was waiting for a full set. Don't ask me how she chewed them off, but she ended up with only two front teeth. The funniest time was when we were at a party and she kept trying to talk to lads from one side of her face. 'I don't have any teeth, Marn!' she kept saying to me. 'I'm never going to pull!' And one time, we were so sex-starved and horny that we even ended up sharing a dildo on screen! That's how mad Chloe is.

Nathan was like a breath of fresh air, too. He said he was bisexual and because I hadn't come out as bisexual then, he became the first in the house to lay claim to that title. Apparently, he fancied both me and Aaron, but I reckoned that was bullshit and it was only Aaron he was after. He'd never actually been with a girl. As far as I know he still hasn't! So I reckon he said he was bisexual because he found all the boys intimidating. There's so much testosterone flying around that place – and that's just the girls!

As for Aaron, I was finding it hard being back in the house with him. On the one hand, I'd go to sleep dreaming of Dan and then, when I was out with Aaron and we got chatting, I wanted a time machine to transport me back to the place where he and I were necking on. I felt so confused. I didn't even like talking to Aaron about Dan for fear I'd cave in and be unfaithful. But every time I got drunk it was like Aaron waved his magic wand and I was right back there, telling him daft things like, 'You're perfect. Why are you so perfect, Aaron?' Arrggghhh! Honestly, when I remember that now, I cringe! I even had to get the girls to enact 'operation code red' to warn me off him when we got too flirty, which was basically them making chicken noises in my ear in the middle of a club. Did it stop me wanting Aaron? No!

What made the situation worse is that Aaron didn't pull anyone for the whole time of filming. Off camera he kept trying to corner me and wear me down, and I'm sure it's because he was jealous I was with Dan. He'd never been this full-on before.

'Marnie, you know how much I like you.'

'I can't, Aaron. You and me has never happened and I'm with Dan now.'

But Aaron went on and on. I genuinely didn't want to hurt Dan. He was a nice lad. Before I'd gone to film we'd had 'the conversation'. Outwardly Dan had been pretty cool knowing I had history with the other lads in the house. Nevertheless, we made a promise to one another.

'Listen, Marn, we need to talk. It's going to be hard being apart but I'll still be here when you come home.'

'It's only four weeks, Dan. We can both be faithful.'

Underneath, though, I think Dan was more paranoid about me getting with Aaron than he let on and I guess he had good reason to be. I did end up taking the piss out of him. At first, I honestly don't think it would have mattered if I'd said to him, 'Dan. I've had sex with Drake!' He always took me back. He was dead sweet, but I also thought, 'What a mug!' He was a nice lad and I was a complete bitch. One hundred per cent I put that show before him.

As filming went on, Aaron really started to get under my skin, and every time we got drunk he always made me think, what if? Then, when we went to Wales with Tash-On Tours, I cracked and kissed him. I even felt bad while I was doing it. I knew it was wrong, but I couldn't help myself. We were all staying in a caravan that night and Aaron and I shared a bed. Nothing happened other than kissing and spooning, but when I woke up the next morning it hit me so hard that I'd cheated on Dan. I felt awful. I might not have counted Dan as serious, but he didn't deserve that. I couldn't stop crying and it got worse when this gorgeous bouquet of red roses turned up from him. In reality, I knew that gesture had probably been prompted by the producers and it was timed to coincide with me cheating on my boyfriend, but it didn't make me feel better.

I had to leave to tell Dan what I'd done and I was dreading hurting him from the moment I left the house. The best thing I could do was come straight out with it, even if it was going to kill me.

'I've cheated on you. I'm so sorry, Dan,' I told him.

'With Aaron?'

Dan knew straight away who I'd been with. And he didn't want anything to do with me. It was horrible because he wasn't even angry, he was just so upset. He came round to Mam's and ended up running out of her front door with me trailing behind on the street crying and shouting to him that I was sorry. I wanted to explain to him about how me and Aaron was unfinished business and how I'd never meant to cheat on him, but he didn't want to know.

'I knew you'd do this, Marnie. I fucking knew you'd do this,' he kept repeating.

'I'm so sorry, Dan. Let me explain.'

'It's over, Marnie. I don't care about an explanation.'

After that there was nothing left to say. Suddenly I felt very alone, like I'd really let myself down. I had really fucked up big time and it reminded me of the time I cheated on my first boyfriend, Glenn. He'd been equally upset and we never spoke again. Exactly the same thing happened with Dan.

I was due to go back into the house the next day, but Anna had arranged for us to go to Hamburg for a few days so I ended up meeting the others at the airport. It was so awkward seeing Aaron. He was really off with me, and we didn't even speak. I thought, I've just told my boyfriend about you, and he's dumped me. Did I do all that for nothing?

Not long after we got to the hotel, Charlotte let on that Aaron had told her he had no intention of being with me. *What the hell?* I was foaming! How could Aaron play around with my feelings like that? Hamburg is probably my worst behaviour in the *Geordie Shore* house. I can't even think about it now without feeling so ashamed over the way I kicked off. But Aaron played around with me so much that it did my head in.

In the club that night, he was being so sly. Off camera he was quietly whispering in my ear to kiss him. He was being dead flirty, making me giggle and encouraging me to get with him. It was scary because Aaron had me like putty in his hands. With him I never felt in control. That night, I went from wanting him to despising him. As soon as my back was turned he was cracking on to these German lasses. I thought, 'For three weeks, you've not spoken to a girl or pulled a girl. You've given me all the attention, and the minute I've cheated on my boyfriend and I'm single, you're not interested!' I figured all he'd wanted to do was get me to cheat and make me look like a bad person. So I charged at him in the club. Utter frustration propelled me across the dance floor. My only goal was to kick the shit out of Aaron – I was like a woman possessed! It took Kyle and Nathan to hold me back.

Hamburg was probably the lowest point for everyone in the house since I'd got there. Me and Aaron weren't speaking – in fact, after the fight Aaron swore on his mam's life that he'd never speak to me again. Charlotte and Gary had also fallen out and Kyle and Holly weren't talking to each other either. World War III had properly kicked off. I reckon the only two people talking were Nathan and Chloe!

This continued way after we got back from Hamburg. After a week, we still weren't speaking. Charlotte and I refused to go out, and Holly went home. I wanted Aaron to admit to me he'd behaved badly and that playing me like a yo-yo was not on, but that was like waiting for the moon to stop setting! The producers kept pulling each of us aside.

'Can we persuade you to talk to Aaron?'

'Nope.'

'We could arrange a meeting where you could both settle your differences.'

'Nah.'

Behind the scenes, the crew were having a right panic, running around saying, 'What the fuck are we going to do?' And I was really depressed when I got back. Now more than ever I felt disgusted at myself for what I'd done to Dan. Especially as I'd cheated with someone who clearly wasn't worth my time. Every moment of that week hurt.

Then Chloe spent the night with Aaron! What the actual fuck? OK, they were fully clothed and spooning on the sofa when I went to the loo one morning after they'd all been out, but even so, Chloe was supposed to be my friend! Even now, the only reason I can fathom why Chloe tried to get with Aaron was to make an impact on TV. And the more impact you make in your first series, the more likely it is that you're in the next. That's just the way TV is. You've got to be thick-skinned to survive it.

Chloe and I did speak about the situation. I was fuming, but I couldn't be too angry with her. I liked Chloe. I probably even fancied her, too. It never happened again between her and Aaron and it's never really affected our friendship. When you make a true friend in that house you have to keep them close.

CHAPTER 15

HEAD OVER HEELS

As soon as filming was over, I wanted to plough myself into other work and I'd started doing a lot more outside of *Geordie Shore*. The girls fare better than the boys when it comes to promoting themselves outside of the show. For example, Charlotte and Holly filmed fitness DVDs and for a time, Vicky wrote a column in a woman's magazine as well as doing other TV. There's always the chance to model clothes or beauty products. And women's magazines feature you, whereas for boys there's less opportunity. Women love to gossip and read about each other. We're always scrolling online, thinking, 'What's Kim Kardashian wearing this week?' And girls are what you'd call more 'press friendly'. Don't get me wrong, there is a downside to that. The pressure on you to be perfect is intense. It's a vicious cycle because the more perfect you are, the more work you get. The industry can be very shallow and soul-destroying like that. And when you stop to think about it, no one's perfect. It's hard not to become consumed by it, though, and you have to take a step back and see it for what it is.

I don't know when, but I know there'll be a day when I'm not in *Geordie Shore* anymore or the show's bubble will burst, and I have to plan for my future.

That's one of the reasons I recently signed up to do an intensive photography course. I love taking photos, especially with my new digital camera, and I want to improve my Instagram page. Plus, I'm enrolled on a beauty course so I can learn to apply make-up professionally. Believe it or not, that's something I've never been able to do. Walking into a classroom after all these years is going to feel very weird, but I keep telling myself that this time it's not school. I'm doing this because I want to do it, so it's different.

Anyway, following series ten I changed agent again. If I'm honest, I still wasn't 100 per cent happy but it was brilliant I was being given more chances to spread my wings. Lasula, an online fashion boutique, had asked me if I wanted to launch my own clothing range. Whaaaaat? I had to pinch myself! Only two years before, I'd been over the moon that I could buy a jumper in Topshop! Now I was launching my own range! I was buzzing! I loved Lasula clothes, too. This was the sort of unimaginable dream I'd had when I was a teenager – up there with duetting with Beyoncé and marrying Leonardo DiCaprio! Crazy, huh?

Surprisingly, I had quite a lot to say about what kind of range I wanted. I'd never been able to afford nice clothes, but I do think I've got a good eye when it comes to style. Loads of girls my age get the piss taken out of them for dressing provocatively so I wanted clothes that didn't make us look like total slappers. Plus, I wanted the range to be affordable. All in all, it had forty-five pieces, from a gorgeous leopard-skin tight dress to jumpsuits and jackets, trousers and tops that you could dress down for the day and dress up in the evening. What I liked most about it was that the designers I worked with understood my style and my personality and ran with it. I also loved modelling the range. The launch night was in Newcastle and being near home made it feel very special.

Whereas before I hadn't been recognised much in the street, now I was being stopped all the time. While I didn't mind some people, others stalked me before they would ever pluck up the courage to ask me for a photo. That was weird! What fans don't understand is that on the show, the volume on everything is turned up – it's so hyper. There're so many arguments and conversations and daft stuff that happens. It's my chance to show the side of myself that's immature and reckless. Admittedly that is a part of me, but it's not me *all the time*. Yet the people who'd started approaching me in the street either wanted to call me a slag or a bitch, which was really upsetting. Or they wanted me to be the Marnie that's mad drunk and necking Jägermeisters and dancing my head off. But sometimes, just sometimes, I wanted to sit with Mam in a coffee shop in Newcastle and talk about normal stuff, like where her and Eric were going on holiday or me buying a house!

Unfortunately, that's the one part of being in the public eye that I've not dealt with very well, and it's changed my personality. I won't even go into a supermarket on my own anymore because I get panic attacks. It's the fans that have made *Geordie Shore* successful and 98 per cent of the time people are so friendly, but every now and again I've literally had to run from places because I've been followed. Everyone's got their own way of dealing with it. For example, Charlotte will let someone trail around her for ages and then she'll tap them on the shoulder and say, 'Do you want a picture?' I can't do that. Instead, I freeze and get very anxious.

My ex-boyfriend, Lewis, always had my back on that score. One time, when we were eating in a restaurant and a person wanted a picture, Lewis said: 'Do you mind? We're eating. Can you give my girlfriend some space?' I thought he was so rude and I wanted the ground to swallow me up. But I loved that he was so manly and protective, too. I can be a bit of a pushover and I would never have said that myself.

What I did enjoy at first was being photographed, which sounds like a bizarre contradiction, but it's true. OK, the paps can be really scary at times. For starters, they are all men and sometimes there can be twenty or more all falling over themselves to get a picture, like a proper scrum. Being chased by photographers has only really happened to me in the last year, and it has made me a bit terrified. At first, though, I did enjoy being on the red carpet at premieres and award ceremonies and doing the PAs that are all part of being on the show.

One of those times was when we were invited to the National Television Awards in London. Other than modelling at Miss Newcastle, I'd never been to a big, posh, black-tie do. And compared to the Civic Centre in Newcastle this was huge! The evening was held at the O2 and *Geordie Shore* was up for the Best Multi-Channel Programme award against *Celebrity Juice* and *Game of Thrones*. Beforehand, we were convinced we were going to win because we'd been tweeting in the weeks running up to the event and, between us, we had millions of followers.

I didn't think much about what I was going to wear. I'd never been to an evening like that before so I was very blasé about it. I put much more effort into my dresses these days because I know the next morning I'll be plastered across the papers whether I like it or not. Now, I look at the pictures of me from that night and cringe. What the fuck was I wearing? At the last minute, I ordered a Jarlo maxi dress off ASOS. Online, I loved it. It had a cream sweetheart neckline with a beautiful embroidered design and white netting below the knee. I even loved it when I tried it on, but the cameras did me no favours. In all the pictures, I look like I'm trying to stop that dress from falling down. And my hair was crimped! I don't know what I was thinking! I do remember stepping into a taxi that night thinking I looked bad and not feeling very confident. And being on a red carpet can be very intimidating. When I was pictured with Scott, Chloe and Nathan there was safety in numbers but on my own I felt very exposed. All these zoom lenses pointing at you and camera flashes and photographers calling over, 'Marnie, can you turn this way?' and 'How are you tonight?' If you are not used to it, it can be very nerve-wracking!

Fortunately, the press were kind to me. The following day, one newspaper even called me 'a vision in white', and said I looked 'glowing'. In fact, all the girls from the show – Charlotte, Holly, Chloe and me – were described as 'demure' on several occasions, which is never a word that's used about us while we're on *Geordie Shore*! But I like to confound people's expectations and show the public thát I can be a different person to the one I am on screen. I do think I should have dressed in an outfit that was a bit more sexy, though!

The actual NTA ceremony is completely mad. It's so weird to be part of a show up in Newcastle and then to arrive at an event in London where everyone you've ever seen off the telly is standing right near to you! I didn't officially brush shoulders with anyone – I was far too shy to stroll up and chat shit to complete strangers – but I was buzzing when I spotted Jeremy Kyle. I absolutely love his show!

When we didn't win, we were fuming! *Celebrity Juice* got the gong but we'd convinced ourselves that we were the better show. What made it worse was that Kris Jenner from *The Kardashians*, who was introducing us, messed it up and didn't say the programme name at the right time, and when she did, she called us *Georgie Shore*! As Keith Lemon bounded up onto the stage, I could feel the cameras pan across us. We all smiled and clapped politely, but underneath we were gutted! Still, I had a great time. Sophie came with us too, even though she wasn't appearing on the show then and she and I danced our heads off in the auditorium after the awards ended. I even took my shoes off so I could bust some moves, but when I went to collect them from under a chair shortly before we carried on to a nightclub, some random had stolen the straps! They were white sandals and the ankle straps were holding them up! How low can you get?

Sophie wanted to go on and party in a club in Soho called Dstrkt, where all the celebrities party.

'I can't go looking like this. I've got a full-on gown and no shoes!' I yelled at Sophie above the music.

'Get in the toilet!' she ordered me.

Both of us were wedged into a cubicle while Sophie ripped the netting off the bottom of my dress. Then she went missing for five minutes and came back armed with two hair bobbles that she'd picked up from God knows where. Now I had a dress that was knee-length but completely jagged at the bottom, and two scraggy bobbles threaded though the tops of my sandals to keep them up. Kim Kardashian I was not!

Soon, I didn't care what I looked like. If I've had a drink all I want to do is party. Anyway, it was too far to go back to the hotel to change. I thought, 'If there're any paps I'll just have to run!' Fortunately, no pictures of me looking mortal with a ripped dress and makeshift shoes have turned up in any newspaper or magazine yet!

The minute we got into Dstrkt we bagged a table and ordered in loads of champagne. Some of the others knew members of the cast from *TOWIE* so they also piled on our table. I'd watched *TOWIE* in the past, but this was the first time I'd actually spoken to anyone who appeared on it. Then Sophie and I hit the dance floor. One guy followed us and came to chat to me – Ricky Rayment. At first, I didn't think he was interested in me, but he was being dead flirty and telling me how lovely I looked. Honestly, that guy must have needed glasses because I'm sure my spray tan had gone all patchy and my mascara was so far down my face that I looked like a sad panda!

'Great to meet you, darlin'' he kept saying. And Ricky was funny because not only was he tall, dark and very handsome, but he had such a strong, London accent. I'd only ever been with Geordie lads before, and they all have short back and sides hair and they aren't smooth like Southern boys. And Ricky was *really* smooth. The first thing I noticed about him was that he had this amazing smile and he was always laughing, and he strutted around the place like he had so much confidence.

I knew that Ricky used to go out with Jessica Wright – Mark Wright's sister – from *TOWIE*. And that made me feel very insecure. I didn't feel in her league at all. She's freakin' gorgeous! I'd always seen her and Ricky pictured together in magazines and she looked tall and so glamorous with a perfect figure and thick brunette hair. She was a proper woman whereas I was definitely rocking the girl-next-door look! And, after my botched nose job, 'the spike' stuck out a mile on my face. I thought, 'How can he fancy me with a huge spike on my face?' But one thing led to another in the club and when we all piled into a taxi and ended up in Stringfellows, we kissed for the first time. I wish now, I hadn't been quite so drunk because I hazily recall that kiss being amazing. Ricky had this soft designer stubble and he was so manly. I was buzzing! But he couldn't hold his drink like Northern lads.

He and I ended up getting another taxi back to my hotel, which was between Piccadilly Circus and Buckingham Palace. It felt so classy stepping out and being welcomed by a porter in a top hat. But the minute we got into my room, Ricky legged it to the toilet to be sick and stayed there on his hands and knees vomiting for an eternity while I passed out fully clothed on the bed. We didn't even kiss or attempt sex! Neither of us was capable!

What was nice, was when I woke up the next morning Ricky was cuddling me. It felt amazing to lie there with my head on his chest. And I was reassured that it hadn't just been the vodka goggles doing the talking! I *really* fancied him. One trip to the bathroom, though, and that warm glow soon faded. When I looked in the mirror my hair was all matted and stank of cigarette smoke. My spray tan was patchier than a giraffe and I had lipstick smeared over my cheeks. When I looked back at Ricky, he looked so fresh whereas I looked like death had run over me twice! God, he really was gorgeous!

It wasn't awkward at all, though. We chatted about the night and how happy we were to have come home together. Immediately, it felt like I'd known him for years! We did not shut up, which I think is a really good sign when you first meet someone. Like me, Ricky seemed very down to earth, although underneath I remember feeling a bit shy. Then we ordered a full English breakfast in bed, got our stuff together, and he waved goodbye to me as I hopped out of a taxi at Kings Cross to get the train back to Newcastle.

Being hungover, that journey seemed to take an eternity, but I kept thinking about Ricky and how lovely he'd been. The problem was, he lived in Essex and I lived in Newcastle so I didn't know if I'd see him again. Before he left me at the station, though, he did take my number. 'This is a good sign,' I thought.

By the time I reached Mam's four hours later, I was dead on my feet.

'Marnie, something's arrived for you,' she said as I walked through the door.

'I'll get it later, Mam. Let me sit down first.'

'No, Marn, go to your room. It's a surprise!'

Mam was pretty insistent and when I turned the corner all I could see was this humongous bouquet of roses. Wow! They were so pretty. The tag read something like, 'Thanks for an amazing night, love Ricky.'

I had no idea how he'd even got my address!

'Mam. I've only just left him!' I shouted. And from that moment on I was hopelessly swept off my feet. Naturally, I texted him 'thank you' and then texting turned into ringing and soon we were talking to each other every night. One thing I noticed about Ricky was he was very full-on. I'm not the sort of person to tell someone I love them straight away. I like to get to know boys first, but Ricky told me he loved me by the end of the first week. Admittedly, I did say it back but mostly because I didn't want to hurt his feelings. I did like him. A lot. But I didn't love him.

He did do the sweetest things, though. Once he spent a whole evening texting me and pretending he was at home, when he was actually en route to Mam's in South Shields. When the doorbell sounded, he was stood there clutching a McDonald's Happy Meal. He knew it was my favourite! I thought, 'This guy's actually driven for four hours to buy me a Happy Meal! I am so lucky!' At times it didn't feel like our 'honeymoon period' would ever end. We clicked. We laughed at the same jokes. We liked the same things. I wondered whether we were actually the same person!

I suppose because both of us were starring in TV series, Ricky was the first public relationship I'd ever had. All my other boyfriends had been from home. At first I liked the attention from the paps. I wanted to show Ricky off and he felt the same about me. We were enjoying getting dressed up and looking good and being seen out together. But social media went crazy. Lots of people started commenting that Jessica was prim and proper and, by comparison, I was a slag. Then pictures started appearing of me and her side by side, only I was mortal, falling down in the street and she was posing in front of a camera looking *A-mazing*. I didn't have a clue who the trolls were but I felt gutted when the press started picking up on it, too.

I'd not met Jess Wright then, but she looked pretty and she seemed like a lovely person on screen, but the newspapers were determined to create this false hatred between us. I thought, 'I don't even know the girl! That's so unfair!' The bottom line was that Jess was older than me, and I found her intimidating. In fact, I met her recently at an industry party and she wasn't scary at all. She's really sweet. Obviously, I think the fact I'm not with Ricky anymore helped, but she wasn't the super-bitch she'd been made out to be. Hopefully, she felt the same about me. We even ended up comparing notes on what a shit boyfriend Ricky turned out to be!

My relationship with Ricky did change me, though. For the first time in a long time I respected the person

I was with. Because we are both in the public eye I didn't want to do anything to embarrass him or hurt him. Funnily, it meant that when I went back into *Geordie Shore* for series eleven, which was filmed in Greece, I made a promise to myself to chill out, not get too drunk, and not do anything stupid with Aaron like I'd done when I was with Dan. It was the first time I was entering the house determined to have fun with the girls . . .

CHAPTER 16

IT'S ALL GREEK TO ME!

When I got to Greece for series eleven, I wasn't the same person I'd been in the *Geordie Shore* house for the last two years. For a start, I missed Ricky like crazy and that was made worse by me losing my phone two days before the show started. Our phones are always confiscated during filming, but sometimes you can wangle it with a crew member to make a secret phone call. Now, I couldn't even do that.

Six weeks away from Ricky was soooooo difficult. I thought about him constantly and I probably sounded like a scratched record, banging on about how much I was into him. Every night when we went out to a club, I thought, 'I wonder where Ricky is now? I wonder if he's out looking at other girls?' Not being

I still love a party, but
getting dressed up for a
night out with the girls
was always the best!

Top: Mam and Eric in Las Vegas – I am so glad that Mam's found someone so good for her. She deserves the best!

Above: Eric really has become one of the family.

Me and Mam mucking about – we're always up for a laugh.

Sophie wasn't happy when I first entered the *Geordie Shore* house, but we'll always be family and that comes first.

Elvis may not be entirely Chihuahua but he's captured my heart!

Elvis and Smyth – my gorgeous double-trouble doggies!

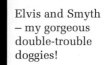

Facing page.
Chloe Goodman
and me

Aaron and I rode a serious rollercoaster when it came to a relationships.

Me and my manager, Craig. I owe so much to him!

Geordie Shore has opened so many doors for me, that I otherwise would never have had. I will never forget that!

Coming out was hard, but I felt so much better for it – there's nothing worse than not being able to express yourself. Doing the shoot for DIVA, I felt so proud to just be myself.

My journey so far has sure been a bumpy ride but I would never have done any of it without my family. Love you all.

But most importantly – Mam, you have been my rock.

able to speak to him made me ultra paranoid and, thankfully, he told me later that he felt the same.

In the house, there was lots and lots of drama, but for once it wasn't my drama. Holly and Kyle, who'd been having an on–off relationship in the show, argued constantly. No joke, there were ten arguments a day on and off screen. They were tearing the house apart. Personally, I thought Kyle was behaving like a massive douchebag. I felt very sorry for Holly and wanted to be there for her as a friend. The problem was that despite Kyle being in a relationship with Holly, he still wanted to go out and pull with the other lads. As far as I'm concerned, when you're in a relationship you make sacrifices.

For the first time ever, it felt like me and the girls bonded. Being with Ricky meant I made an effort. I wasn't on the pull or chasing after Aaron, or even that bothered about what he was doing or who he was doing it with. In fact, whenever I looked at him, I didn't feel anything. It was like someone had waved a magic wand and his spell had finally been lifted. He was a nightmare drunk, though – always grabbing my face and trying to kiss me. All I kept thinking was, 'What if Ricky sees this when it airs? I don't want to upset him!'

As it turned out, Ricky and I weren't together when the series finally aired in October 2015. That was weird! When I watch those episodes now, I realise that travelling to Greece with the show was one of the happiest times I've spent with the housemates. I bonded with the girls 100 per cent. But I do find it difficult being reminded of Ricky. Some of it's pure cringe! I was pining over him like a lovesick teenager.

Never having been to Greece before, I was so excited, and the first apartment that Anna had fixed up for us in Zante was mint. Outside there was this huge pool shaped like a love heart surrounded by sun loungers. At times, I had to pinch myself and think, 'I'm getting paid to sunbathe!'

During the series, there were loads of pool parties and going out clubbing, but at times I didn't even drink. It was like the Virgin Mary had taken over my mind and body. Everybody commented on it! 'Marnie, what's happened? You're as dull as a school teacher!'

Thankfully, glimpses of the old me appeared every so often. Halfway through the series, Chloe and I had our first lesbian experience and I'm sure it was because I was so sex-starved not seeing Ricky. We'd all been out to a bar. I was mortal and Chloe was in an even worse state, falling around all over the place. In the minibus home to the villa, we started kissing and one thing led to another and soon we were scissoring in the passenger seat! Only the lads were with us and Gary kept grabbing the camera and filming us like we were in some lesbian porno! They thought it was hilarious and everyone was shouting and clapping. The more they encouraged us, the more we necked on.

At the time, we thought it was dead sexy and cool. But the next morning? I didn't feel so clever. First of all, the camera guy with us was really fit, and I was so embarrassed by what had happened that every time he walked into the villa the next day I had to turn around and walk out.

'Please, please don't use the footage,' I begged the producers.

'We have to, Marnie!' they told me, which made me kick off even more.

'I'm leaving then. Put me on a flight back to Newcastle!'

I burst out crying and begged them. Part of the reason I was so mortified was because I was with Ricky and I didn't want to do anything to end the relationship. Although I'd kissed girls before, I'd not properly explored that part of my sexuality. Now, I didn't know what I was! Was I straight? Was I gay? It was the first time something really full-on had happened with me. If I'm honest, it was a bit of a head-fuck!

It was such a relief when I learned later that after the producers had gone through the tape they decided the scenes between me and Chloe were too explicit to be used. In the end, they only showed us kissing on screen. I was so happy! And even though I commented afterwards that that was my first and last proper lesbian experience, it's definitely not been my last. I don't think twice about kissing Chloe now. She's a really good kisser, better than most lads. She's a legend! She's one of my fun friends who I can get physical with and I know it'll never get serious. The way I see it is I have girlfriends I can kiss and girlfriends I wouldn't dream of kissing! For instance, I wouldn't kiss Holly or Charlotte, even though Charlotte and I have had one drunken kiss on the show.

In total, we visited five islands in Greece – Zante, Corfu, Crete, Mykonos and Ios as well as Athens on the mainland. I loved Greece, and I especially loved the yacht that took us to each island. Lying on deck with the sun beating down and being able to jump off into the clear blue water was amazing. I felt like I was on the set of a film! Below deck it was a different story. Although the boat looked huge from the outside, it was really poky inside. The steps down to the bedrooms were very narrow and all four girls were squeezed into one room. It was so hot at night, we thought we were going to die!

Then the toilet got blocked by Nathan and we couldn't use it. That was rank! Nathan is well known for pooing all the time in the house – I think he has irritable bowel syndrome and, no joke, he must poo around fourteen times a day. Whenever we need to get out of the house, we are always late because Nathan is pooing. He's like this human poo factory! On the boat, it was a nightmare. The only place we could wee was off the deck or into a bucket and no one wanted to poo at all. Eventually Charlotte cracked and took it upon herself to unblock the loo. She's braver than all of us put together because we wouldn't go near it! She took a deep breath, yanked on some rubber gloves, stuck her hand in and scooped out all the shit into a plastic bag. All of us girls were peeping round the bathroom door, laughing our heads off and shouting encouragement to her. She couldn't stop retching. Poor Charlotte! It was so disgusting that I don't think they showed poo policewoman Charlotte on TV. It was such a low moment!

In addition to this, Kyle and Holly's arguments reached a level that none of us could bear and Kyle ended up leaving. The minute he went, it was like a dark cloud had been lifted. Calm had been restored. It felt good that for once I could be there for Holly. She needed many, many shoulders to cry on. She must have cried every night for weeks.

But towards the end of our time in Greece, I had a funny feeling something was afoot and that drama would land on my doorstep soon. On one of our down nights in Zante something really strange happened. Usually we have a crew member looking after us on those nights. We don't go out and we don't drink and it's our chance to rejuvenate. But we're still not allowed to use our phones. Sometimes the show's producers even turn up to spy on us, but as we were in a villa in the middle of nowhere, that was unlikely to happen. James, the crew member looking after us, let the others use their phones, but as I'd lost mine I borrowed Charlotte's. I was so desperate to talk to Ricky. I'd missed him and I wanted to hear his voice.

'Hi, it's Marnie!'

'Hello, darling,' he replied, but he didn't sound happy to hear from me.

'Let's FaceTime. I can't wait to see you.'

'We can't. The connection won't work. I've got to go, babe. Talk soon.'

'Well, I'm ringing you now and the connection's fine!'

I couldn't understand why Ricky didn't want to carry on the conversation. He'd acted really odd. Immediately, I thought the worst. He'd met someone. He didn't want to be with me anymore. What if a girl was with him when I'd called?

Charlotte's phone was still in my hand when, minutes afterwards, the door to the girls' bedroom flung open and James rushed in.

'Give me the phones! Give me them all.' He was fuming.

'What the hell's happened?'

'I am in so much shit. Your boyfriend's grassed me up!'

'*What the hell?*'

His behaviour was so peculiar, and when I thought about it I couldn't help wondering whether Ricky was in Greece. How exactly did Ricky grass James up? I later learned that the minute Ricky had put the phone down on me he rang one of the show's directors and told her we'd spoken. She'd phoned James. 'Why's Marnie got Charlotte's phone?'

Unbeknown to me Ricky *had* arranged with the producers to come out. Being abroad had made me realise how in love I was with him and my sixth sense told me something was about to happen. I could barely sleep that night, I was so anxious.

Sure enough, the next day, while we were all sunbathing by the pool, a silver taxi pulled up.

'Who's that?' everyone was looking.

Out jumped Ricky in his shorts and T-shirt armed with a bouquet of flowers. I was buzzing! I remember leaping off the sun lounger in my bikini and legging it towards him shouting, 'Oh my God, it's my boyfriend, Ricky!'

Seeing his face was mint. He was even more handsome than I'd remembered and with his shades on he looked almost Greek! I jumped up on him and hugged him so tightly. I couldn't help thinking this was the most romantic thing anyone had ever done for me, and that he must really love me to have come all this way. It was so surreal.

Not long after he arrived, Ricky told me he was going to get changed and that he'd pick me up in a taxi and take me into the mountains for a drink in a couple of hours. I was so made up to be going on a date with him again, but I did have this weird feeling, like something was about to happen. Ricky's parents lived in Florida and he'd travelled all the way from the States to Zante. No one does that just for the hell of it, do they?

The taxi took me to a secluded restaurant up in the mountains where Ricky was waiting. We had a drink and talked. I even told Ricky that I couldn't get his willy out of my mind. I couldn't, though! It's all I'd thought about for weeks!

'I've got a surprise for you,' he announced after an hour or so, before leading me to the cliff top and covering my eyes with his hands.

'Oh my God, what the hell's he doing?' I thought. I had this funny feeling that Ricky was about to propose, but I put it out of my head. I'd missed him, but we'd only been going out for six weeks. I had no idea if I wanted to spend the rest of my life with him!

He launched into this huge speech about growing old together and how he loved everything about me. Then he asked me to turn and look over the cliff to the beach. Metres below a huge heart had been carved out in the sand, and all these bamboo firelights spelled out 'Marry Me' with a big question mark at the end.

Then he got down on one knee and presented me with the ring. Inside, I was squirming. I thought, no, no, no please don't do this! It was amazing and beautiful, and very dramatic, but I felt surprisingly overwhelmed.

When the series finally aired, the camera shows me eventually saying, 'Yes' after thirty seconds of me not knowing what the hell to say. What the viewers didn't see was me legging it to the top of the hill in floods of tears.

'He told me he was taking me for a drink. I feel so confused!' I was screaming to Nia, the programme director.

All the time, I was thinking, 'I don't want to be a wife! I'm not ready for that!' And didn't Ricky think that maybe I would have wanted all of my friends and family at my engagement? He'd arrived on my last night in Greece but why hadn't he waited until filming had ended and proposed to me privately?

The other problem for me was I had a feeling that Ricky hadn't done any of it. I couldn't believe that he'd arranged the drink or the lights on the beach. It felt like *Geordie Shore* was proposing to me, not Ricky. But later, I found out he'd been sending pictures of engagement rings to people from the show. He knew that if he rang the programme with the idea of an engagement then they'd jump on it as a dramatic twist to the end of the season. For me, none of it felt real!

All sorts of other scenarios were running through my mind, too. I even figured that maybe Ricky wanted me off the show and that's why he'd asked me. Realistically, I wasn't going to walk down the aisle with my fiancé and then be able to continue getting palatic and going out clubbing with the housemates in *Geordie Shore*. The bottom line was he was asking me to choose between them or him. It was so unfair!

Also, Ricky's proposal made me think that maybe he didn't know me after all. *Geordie Shore* is like being in one big family, and I'd only just started to find my feet. Now I love each and every one of those housemates in different ways and we've all shared a unique experience together. Given how much of an outsider I'd felt in the house when I started, giving it up wasn't going to be easy. Ricky didn't seem to understand that.

'We tried to make the proposal really special,' Nia pleaded with me.

'I know. I'm in a new relationship with him, but that doesn't mean I want to be married!'

I felt so responsible about my decision. And when I looked at Ricky's face he looked gutted, like I'd punctured his heart. Then I looked at the ring. It was silver and gold with a large diamond in the middle. I kept thinking how beautiful it was. If I said no, I knew Ricky would finish with me there and then. I didn't want to stop going out with him, I just didn't want to marry him! After some contemplating, I eventually said yes on screen, but inside I felt so conflicted. I couldn't help feel I was making a major decision because I wanted it to fit the show, not because it fitted my life.

Later, when we went to join the others in the club, I still felt torn. One part of me was buzzing but the other was thinking, 'Why the hell am I celebrating my engagement in a night club?' It actually felt quite sleazy and when we got back to the house I was so mortal that Ricky and I couldn't have sex properly. I didn't even take my clothes off. That's not what I'd wanted at all!

The next morning after Ricky left, I knew I'd have to tell the others that I was leaving Greece with him and I wouldn't be coming back. It was such a hard choice to make and I couldn't stop bawling my eyes out. When it came to my announcement, I couldn't keep it together at all. As the words were coming out it felt like my heart was being ripped out as well. Even Aaron gave me a massive goodbye hug and the pain of leaving everyone hit me so hard.

Had that decision been two years ago, I wouldn't have cared, but now the house felt special. We had a proper bond and I thought of Holly, Charlotte and Chloe as my sisters.

But before I could go and meet Ricky at his hotel, I

had to film my final green screen. I made everyone cry! Every time I spoke, I kept breaking down in tears and setting the crew off, too. In my head, I was thinking, 'What am I doing? I don't want to leave all this behind!'

At Ricky's hotel, I walked in looking like I'd been dragged through a hedge backwards. My eyes were swollen and I could barely look at him. He was outside smoking when I arrived and he looked at me and shrugged. 'Sorry, babe,' he said, smiling. I could feel the resentment bubbling up inside. Sadly, my engagement turned out to be the high point of knowing Ricky.

CHAPTER 17

BROKEN DREAMS

The minute I left *Geordie Shore,* and Ricky and I left Greece, was the minute our relationship changed. At first, I wasn't sure whether it was because I still felt furious that Ricky had taken the programme away from me, or whether he'd had some sort of personality transplant. When we landed back in the UK, Ricky said that he didn't want me partying too hard. In fact, he didn't want me going out at all. Everything I did made him jealous. It was like he didn't trust me. I thought, 'What kind of start to an engagement is this?'

'Let's get tattoos done together,' he suggested one day. I wasn't keen on the idea but I went along with it to please him. He had an 'M' inked on his wrist and I had an 'R'. What I was discovering was that Ricky was very good at these full-on displays of affection. He loved flowers and taking me out for meals, but underneath he wasn't the person I thought he was. In private, he was impatient and moody and, at times, very unkind.

I noticed his impatience more after I went to get the scar revision done on my boobs and to have my nose corrected by Dr Hasan. Following the operations I stayed with Ricky in Brentwood in Essex where he has a flat. I was bed-bound with bandages on my boobs and a splint on my face, but from day one he made it obvious he didn't want to look after me. Everything I said or did annoyed him and he acted as if I was a burden to him. If I asked him to get me a glass of water he tutted and made a fuss. All he wanted to do was hang out with his mates.

'The lads are coming over to play PlayStation,' he casually announced one day.

'My eyes are black and blue. I've got shooting pains in my boobs and I'm out of it on medication. Please can you wait before inviting your mates round?'

'No, babe, it's just some mates coming round for a lads night.'

I figured that if the relationship was so important to Ricky then he would have respected my wishes, but instead he sulked like a child. All of a sudden, he was being so inconsiderate. He wanted rid of me and he wasn't even hiding it!

What I'd also noticed about Ricky was how spoiled he was by his family. Don't get me wrong, his mam and dad are lovely – I'd met them a few times when they'd come over from Florida – but they doted on him and gave him everything he wanted. Other than *TOWIE*, I don't think Ricky had ever really needed to work. He couldn't understand why *Geordie Shore* was so important to me. The show was my life and my job but he didn't care. At times I thought he was being a complete dickhead!

On occasions, we had terrible arguments. Thank God Ricky wasn't ever physically violent, but he was violent with his words. He'd say awful things. One time, he said he was only with me because of the sex, and I didn't even do that very well. I was mortified! At other times, he'd ring me mam and bleat on to her about how we weren't getting on – as if Mam was going to take his side. One time I tried to hang the phone up on him and Mam, but he got really angry and started shouting. He mistakenly thought Mam wasn't on the line anymore, but suddenly we heard, 'Marnie? Marnie? Are you there? Are you OK?' drifting up from the receiver. Mam was so worried that he might flip and after that she rang me all the time to check up on me. Her opinion of Ricky changed. She hated him and told me she wasn't keen on me going out with him. As usual, I couldn't see the writing on the wall.

Not long after my operation, I was invited to do a public appearance in a club in Italy. Although I was not planning on going back to the house, I was still made to feel part of the team and I'd missed the others so much that I couldn't wait to be back with my *Geordie Shore* family again. And it was very rare that all the housemates got to do a PA together, especially one that paid £3,000 each! There was no way I was going to turn down that kind of money! And PAs can be good fun. There's always a DJ or entertainment and we get to hang out in the VIP area. Sometimes we have to take the microphone and shout out to the crowd and that can be really nerve-wracking. Occasionally, I refuse, but if I do take the mic, I shout things like, 'Are you all having a good time? It's great to be here!' I still think it's mental that people would go to a club because I'm appearing. Without doubt, the worst PA I've ever done was when I got a bottle of piss thrown at me. It was disgusting. Mostly people are really lovely, though, and just want to hang out with you, have their photo taken with you or get you to sign something. But occasionally you do encounter some complete douchebags.

The event in Italy was held in a huge super-club in Milan. We were all buzzing and drinking and dancing. For the first time in ages, I felt like I was exactly where I wanted to be. When I think about it now, I must have been so unhappy underneath. I'm not making excuses for my behaviour, but the minute I saw Aaron all these feelings came flooding back. I couldn't explain it. In Greece I didn't care about him. I'd packed all that emotion away in a box. I'd met Ricky and we'd moved on. Now, though, it was like someone had opened the lid and I felt this uncontrollable urge to kiss him.

As the night went on and we were in the VIP area, Aaron told me that seeing me with Ricky and me leaving the programme had made him realise he'd lost me.

'I can't go back there, Aaron. You mess with my head and I don't understand it,' I confessed.

'But, Marnie, I've realised that I want you.'

What the hell? Was Aaron admitting he wanted to be with me? I didn't know whether to believe him or not. We'd been through this routine before. Aaron was brilliant at reeling me in and then shutting the door in my face. I didn't want to be hurt by him again. We ended up kissing on the dance floor, but it was just a kiss. My head was in bits. What the hell was I going to say to Ricky?

As it turned out, I didn't have to say anything to him. Not long after I arrived back in Newcastle, I got woken up at four a.m. with a message from him. He'd posted a video of me kissing Aaron in the club that some random had sent him over Facebook. I watched it horrified. It was a full-on passionate kiss. Then he rang me. I didn't know whether to answer or not, I felt so ashamed. The weird thing was that when I did pick up the phone, Ricky wasn't angry. He seemed to me just *really* weird.

As soon as he put the phone down, I received another message. They were so gross and graphic I can't even bear to think about them. *Please!* If Ricky was going to profess his undying love for me, I wanted him to send me flowers and champagne, not this!

Despite all of that, I did agree to go and see him the next day. You're probably thinking why the hell would I do that? But I genuinely wanted to sort things out. And, believe it or not, I did want to have sex with him. Looking back, I sexually matured with Ricky. We had brilliant sex and, because I'd been so into him at the beginning, I felt like I could loosen up and let myself go.

He was not comfortable with me kissing girls, though. He told me on enough occasions. When I finally came out as bisexual, I read an interview with him where he said he wasn't surprised. 'Marnie's a very sexual person. She doesn't mind if it's with a boy or a girl.' I actually felt quite hurt by that because Ricky is a very sexual person. And we were both having that sex – not just me!

Anyway, from the minute I arrived sex was the last thing we did. Instead, we argued so badly that I even threatened to leave him, which sent him over the edge. I'd recently bought a gorgeous chihuahua who I'd named Smith. He was newly born and living in Ricky's flat. That poor dog! In the heat of the argument, Ricky picked him up in his doggy bag and lobbed him at me!

I should have gone home there and then, but the following evening I was doing another PA at a club in London called Gaslight – a posh pole-dancing club in Mayfair. Ricky insisted on coming, but throughout the night he was necking Jägerbomb after Jägerbomb. He was so off with me that I wished he'd go home. All I wanted was to do my job and have a fun time with the others. That night we were staying in a hotel in Mayfair but I didn't know whether I wanted to leave with Ricky – he was being so verbally aggressive.

As we started walking to the hotel we were both drunk but Ricky was barely able to stand and he was shouting all sorts of abuse at me – so much so that passers-by were asking me if I was OK and if I needed them to ring the police. Instead of leaving Ricky to it, I ended up protecting him! I begged one man not to call the police but someone must have dialled 999 anyway because within ten minutes a panda car had pulled up and an officer was stepping out, asking me if Ricky was bothering me. Again, I stuck up for him!

The police officer asked if I was okay and I said I

was fine and that it had been a long night and we were just having an argument.

I was so embarrassed. I wanted the ground to swallow me up. I was also dreading someone recognising us and waking up to a story plastered across the papers. Fortunately, that didn't happen, but I was so shocked that in reality our relationship ended there and then.

The next day I knew what I had to do. Telling Ricky our relationship was over was going to be very painful. Only two months before he'd been on a cliff top in Zante proposing to me, and now I could barely look at him. I disliked him so much. But it was a relief, too. I'd asked Mam and Eric to come and pick me up from Brentwood and I cleared my things from Ricky's flat. He sat there in silence the whole time. I'd got this strength from somewhere, and there was nothing he could say to change my mind or win me back.

When I saw Mam, I was so happy. Whatever goes wrong in my life, she and Eric are my one constant. Ricky was like this whirlwind, but I fell out of love with him as quickly as I'd fallen in love. After we split, I didn't hear from him again. Well, that's until he contacted me to ask for the engagement ring back. Apparently, he was broke and needed the money. I even read interviews with him banging on about me refusing to give it back. I thought, 'Have you got no shame?'

'Ricky, you put me through so much shit that I'm

keeping it,' I told him. Then I started thinking that maybe he wanted it back because it was really valuable. Sadly not! Although he may have paid more for it when I took it to a jeweller he said I wouldn't get loads for it. I couldn't believe he was arguing with me over this ring. Did he really want it back because he needed the money or was he terrified people would find out how little he'd spent on it? I still have the ring today.

Then he had a go at me for officially announcing our split on Twitter. All I said was that I was heartbroken and it was the end of a very important chapter in my life. I didn't slag him off and I was very respectful, but he tweeted in response: 'It amazes me how even the most private of things are a priority to be tweeted #thisisourgeneration'. That made me choke. Hadn't Ricky been the one to propose to me on TV? You couldn't get more public than that!

Ricky had turned from a husband-to-be into a complete arsehole, and when I bumped into him last year I knew that I'd made the right decision. James Locke from *TOWIE* was having an opening for his deli in Romford and I'd gone with Mike Hassini, who is also on the programme and who I was having a brief fling with at the time. One minute I was sitting on Mike's knee kissing him and the next I felt this shadow over me. Jesus! It was Ricky. Then it got worse. I looked to my left and there was Vicky

Pattison. She was the last person I wanted to bump into. After all our arguments in the house, I'd never wanted to set eyes on her again. I had to get out of there! Weirdly, Ricky ended up following us from place to place and even to the late-night strippers. 'Is he that desperate?' I thought.

'You look amazing,' he said to me when we did finally say hello. I thought, 'That's nice, Ricky, but you had your chance and you blew it. I've moved on!'

CHAPTER 18

FINALLY, IT'S HAPPENED TO ME!

Throughout this book, I've gone on about having a guardian angel. Whenever I've been feeling lost or unhappy – *shazam!* Someone amazing appears. And this time it was a new agent who landed on my doorstep.

I've mentioned that I'd never gelled with any of my management, and in 2014 I finally realised we weren't right for each other. Lots of the girls from *Geordie Shore* go on to do fitness DVDs, but their choice isn't necessarily my choice. But my then-management found that hard to understand. Normally production companies target people who are a bit chubby anyway. For example Charlotte was more than eleven stone when she filmed her *3 Minute Belly Blitz* DVD.

I remember talking to her about it and she *wanted* to lose the weight. And when she dropped three stone, she looked mint! But I was never that chubby – I was always between a size eight and ten. I thought, all you want is to make a quick buck out of me rather than consider my health or my long-term career! The problem with fitness DVDs – and not many people know this – is that often you have to gain weight first before you're put on a diet and a hard-core fitness regime so the before and after pictures look dead dramatic. The problem was, I didn't want to be plumped up like a Christmas turkey and I was worried that kind of extreme diet would impact on my health.

Ever since I was a teenager, I've suffered with horrendous bladder problems. Getting mortal in the *Geordie Shore* house doesn't exactly help, but I do try to be careful and stay off the booze for bouts of time. No joke, I only need to blink and I've got an infection downstairs, so I don't go anywhere without loads of multivitamins. Mam's always sending me books about my condition, which is called interstitial cystitis, or IC for short. I'm in so much pain a lot of the time, it's hard to believe I've only got a mild form of the condition. When I was younger, I used to take antibiotics but it got to the point where I was becoming immune. So I found these vitamins online and they do help, though constantly living out of a suitcase can be a nightmare and I go into a right panic if I've forgotten my pills. I change my diet to alleviate the symptoms, too. Recently, though, I had to have an operation on my bladder to stretch it. After months of being in complete agony, I'm starting to feel a bit better.

I've got loads of food intolerances as well. Seriously, I'm a walking nightmare! I'm allergic to gluten, wheat, yeast, milk, carrots and cashews. I mean, who the fuck is allergic to carrots? It had to be me, didn't it?

Anyway, that means getting hot and sweaty in a leotard and eating a lettuce leaf a day isn't going to be good for me. I'm sure my management thought I was being a right diva, but sometimes you have to put your foot down and say that your well-being comes above what any TV company or brand want you to do.

In the meantime, I'd made friends with Chloe Goodman from Ex-on-the-Beach and Celebrity Big Brother. I love Chloe. She's a model and she's dead feisty and we bumped into each other at events. She also hated Vicky Pattinson, so naturally we bonded over that! She had this brilliant agent called Craig who she recommended, and the first time we met we hit it off immediately, so I signed with him. Now, I'm not saying Craig and I didn't have a few tricky moments to start with. Anyone who's watched me in *Geordie Shore* knows I can be headstrong. At first, there were definitely times when I got too drunk and I wouldn't turn up for my appointments or I'd cancel last minute or Craig couldn't get hold of me. Or we'd go out and I'd have an early appointment the next day and I'd refuse to go home because I wanted to carry on getting mortal.

'Marnie, you've got a nine a.m. meeting. Let's get a taxi and go.'

'No! I'm staying out. I'm having fun! Why are you being such a killjoy?'

'Marnie, you're pissed and you'll thank me in the morning.'

'Fuck off, Craig. I'm not getting in a taxi and I'm not going home!'

It's amazing Craig wanted to manage me after that, but he did. I'd even pass my drinks to him to hold if we were out together. That doesn't sound like the crime of the century, but Craig is a recovering alcoholic. He's actually an amazing person because he's been sober for two years. Looking back, I was so insensitive!

'Hold that for two minutes while I get something out of my bag,' I'd shout, passing him my vodka coke.

'*Marnie*,' he'd reply through gritted teeth.

Craig has a way with me that really works – he understands me. I find him such a positive person to be around and he helps me make the right choices. He's not heavy like a school teacher – he's a mate too. If I'm having a shit day, he'll come over and we'll watch box sets together and we'll climb under the duvet and eat crap food, just like me and Mam used to when I was young. Sometimes I have to pinch myself. I'm so lucky that Craig and I found each other. To have someone who is my agent but also my best friend means it's a really special relationship. Because of him, I now understand what it's like to have a great role model. Apart from my family, I know Craig is looking out for me and guiding me in the right direction.

And thanks to Craig I got to go back into *Geordie Shore.* Obviously, when I became engaged to Ricky I left the series; now I was single again I was desperate to go back. But I didn't know if I could. The problem was that by the time Ricky and I split they'd already started filming the next show. Amazingly, the producers agreed that I could go back halfway through on one condition –I wasn't allowed to tell a soul. And I'm dead happy I did go back. Of all the series I've done, series twelve is definitely my favourite. It was sooooo hard keeping my arrival to myself, though.

In between, I'd been doing some promo work and everybody would ask me about being in the house. 'I'm so gutted not to be going back,' I'd tell them. Then the housemates kept messaging me.

'Are you coming back, Marn?'

'No. Totally gutted. Tried my hardest to come back in but I can't . . .'

Lying was hard, but I was so excited to see their

reaction. To this day, returning to the house is a brilliant memory. All the housemates had been to Hull and they were so hungover and pissed off when they walked through the door. They had faces on them like they'd been to a funeral and I could hear them moaning about what a shit time they'd had. All the time I was hiding in the girls' bedroom upstairs. I later learned that the trip had been a disaster because it had all kicked off with new housemate Chantelle Connelly. The minute everyone was in, I chose my moment. Then I appeared at the top of the stairs. 'Hi!' I screamed. Oh my God, the girls went mental. I was buzzing! They legged it halfway up the stairs and there was a massive pile-on. Everyone was on top of me and I could barely breathe! The hilarious thing was that no one gave a shit that my engagement to Ricky was off. In fact, when I told them, they were pleased. All anyone cared about was that I was back in the *Geordie Shore* family. Such a special moment! Chloe told me I'd made her life by coming back. The best thing was that Aaron was buzzing too, and that made me feel so amazing. Almost losing me to Ricky had noticeably changed the way he behaved towards me. For ages, Aaron had played mind games with me so I kept telling myself I needed to remain on my guard. Did he want to be with me? Didn't he? We had *still* never ever shagged! Crazy, huh?

Aaron didn't take long to disappoint! Shortly after

I arrived, I learned he'd had the new housemate Chantelle's name tattooed on his wrist. What the actual fuck? Later, when I watched Aaron back on green screen he said he'd done it because I was engaged, and he'd wanted to pull Chantelle. He also wanted to piss off Scott because Chantelle had wanted to get with him as well. I thought, 'It's one thing fancying a lass, but getting her name tattooed on you before you've even had sex with her isn't just desperate, it's nuts!' Even Aaron admitted that was one tattoo too many! And he'd shagged some random friend of Nathan's in the shag pad while I was away. That didn't bother me as much. I was engaged at the time, and I was probably never going to meet the girl. Probably . . .

With me back in the house, though, Aaron's attention had definitely shifted. He was so full-on and very touchy-feely. When I was with Ricky I'd shut out how I felt about Aaron, now I had this weird feeling whenever he came near me. You know – that nervous feeling in your stomach when you *really*, *really* fancy someone! On my first night back, Aaron and I were flirting in the club and all the others started shouting 'Kiss her! Kiss her!' I was so embarrassed, but there was something that felt right about it, too, like our stars had never been aligned, and now they were about to collide!

When I thought about it, it was actually the first

time Aaron and I had spent time together properly. I was single. He was single. What was stopping us? Well, I don't know the answer to that. I even kept saying to him off camera, 'Why don't you just shag me?' But he wouldn't reply. There was only one thing for it. I was going to have to drop the L-bomb!

I got my chance when we had a house party to welcome new housemate Marty. Admittedly, I wasn't looking my sexiest. I was dressed in a fluffy rabbit onesie and Aaron had a chipmunk outfit on. Feeling hot, hot, hot? Not . . . It may have been the vodka goggles but he looked gorgeous.

I even tried to play it cool when the random Aaron had brought back to the shag pad turned up. I'd banked on never meeting her so I was squirming inside, but Aaron's expression said it all. He looked like he'd seen a ghost. To give him his dues, he pulled me aside and told me who she was and said that he wasn't interested. It didn't make the situation easier. She was walking around all night flaunting her massive tits. I couldn't escape them, like they were following me round the room! At one point, she made me feel so insecure that I shouted to her, 'Go home!' Inside, I was going to explode! I thought, only Aaron could do that to me. Then he tried to calm me down; he was like a different person. He actually started to open up. There he was, telling me that from the minute he'd seen me on my first night back at the top of the stairs, all he wanted was to be with me and not pull other girls.

'Do you want to be single and go on the pull?' he asked me.

'Nah. I love ya.'

I could not stop laughing. What had I just said? I've said a lot of batshit crazy stuff in that house, but this topped the lot. We'd been dancing around each other for eons and I go and tell Aaron I love him. *What the fuck?*

I looked directly into his eyes, terrified of what he might say or do next.

'I really like . . .'

'Come on, Aaron,' I was thinking. 'After all this time, please, please tell me you love me back.'

'. . . I like your hair!'

Hair? Did I hear that correctly? Aaron *really liked my hair*? What kind of a line was that? I didn't know whether to laugh or cry!

Right, I thought, that's not good enough. I'm going to put my pride aside and *beg* Aaron to tell me he loves me.

'I said I love you, and you've told me you like my hair! You don't love me. Tell me you love me!'

'I love you.'

Thank God for that! I thought he was never going to say it. That night, Aaron made me such a happy bunny, but he still wouldn't have sex with me!

Instead, he came up with some excuse that I was too mortal and he wanted me to remember the first time we ever shagged. Shit! The next day, I was grateful, though, and I did think that was very sweet of him. But the fact remained. We still hadn't had sex. Double shit!

The next time we had our chance, I was too sober and it didn't happen then either. The problem was that, being sober, I became so self-conscious about my hairy foof I didn't want Aaron's cock anywhere near it, or even his fingers! Some girls wouldn't have cared, but I'm quite particular when it comes to my fairy. Ever since I was young I've always been very hairy, and it's dark hair too − it's like wearing a tarantula. I've had laser treatment, the lot, but nothing seems to work. Ask any lad if they like a hairy vagina and they always reply 'no'. A lad's got to be a bit weird to want a rumble in the jungle, I reckon.

I shave every other day now. If I could, I would shave every day, but it stings too much so my boyfriends do have to put up with my spiky vagina.

The hilarious thing is that when I was at secondary school, all the girls used to brag about getting pubes and I was desperate for them. Now, I can't wait to get rid of them! Shaving my body is a full-time job. Since I was around fourteen I've been dealing with my hairy arms, legs, belly, armpits and vagina. I'm even going to try laser treatment on the sides of my face because

I am literally growing sideburns. I cannot think of anything more unattractive than a girl with proper bushy sideburns!

After so much toing and froing, when it did finally come to sampling Aaron's willy, it turned out to be another disaster. Everyone thinks that me and Aaron had sex for the first time when we returned to the house for the *Big Birthday Battle*, but we didn't! The first time we ever got it on was in series twelve. I swear to God someone in the *Geordie Shore* crew lost their job the following day because our christening of the shag pad is nowhere to be found on tape.

On the last night, Aaron and I had a date set up for us in Kaspas ice cream parlour. After hitting a club later, we ended up all over each other back at the house. Oh my God! It was amazing – that sex was a total knee-trembler! I couldn't believe we'd waited. Not only was Aaron gentle, but he made me come so many times it was embarrassing. Only, behind the scenes, some idiot in the control room had forgotten to press record! The producers had waited so long for us to seal the deal. They'd stretched the storyline out longer than an elephant's dick. Now they'd fucked up and totally missed the climax! Literally.

The only reason I found out was because the next day we asked the crew what they were going to show of me and Aaron having sex. We were so happy we could finally move the story on! But the look of panic on their faces was priceless ... Shit! Half an hour later, they confirmed that no one had turned the fixed cameras on, and so we were going to have to stick with the Marnie-and-Aaron-have-never-shagged storyline. Jeeezzz! I was pissing myself laughing but Aaron was so angry! All the shots of us leaving the house are of the housemates commiserating with us. 'Maybe you'll get lucky next time, guys.' It was all a big fat lie. 'Yeah, maybe next time,' Aaron shouted back through gritted teeth.

So, the first time Aaron and I officially had sex with the cameras running was when we started filming for the *Big Birthday Battle* series – which was the reunion mini-series where almost everybody turned up from the past. James came back from Australia and Kyle also turned up. Charlotte and Gary got it together ... again! The best surprise was Sophie returning to the show. After everything we'd been though, I was made up to have Sophie back with no bad blood between us whatsoever. We call the housemates in *Geordie Shore* our family, but Sophie's my real family and nothing should ever break that bond.

We did so many stupid things, it was brilliant. For example, dressing up like Stone-Age characters and holding a dinosaur party was one of my highlights. Plus, almost having sex with Aaron dressed as a hillbilly in the kitchens of Madame Koo's nightclub was hilarious. Anna wasn't very pleased about that and she claimed she'd had to have industrial cleaners in to hose down the worktops!

Sadly, me and Aaron getting serious went off the rails almost straight away. Considering how we'd danced around each other for two years, he wasn't keen to commit. It was blatantly obvious he wanted sex but not much else, and that was very disappointing. It was not how I expected our relationship to be at all. What I realised about Aaron was that he didn't know how to treat a girlfriend. He didn't want to put any effort in whatsoever – he just wanted to go out with his mates. I decided to see if he might change, but underneath I made a resolution that I wasn't going to rely on him. If true love happened, it happened, but if someone lovely came along in the meantime then Aaron wasn't going to stop me from going there.

Luckily, I was so busy, I didn't have too much time to dwell on things. Not long after we finished filming, I was due in Australia for ten days of promotions. It was such a good time and the brilliant part was I was allowed to take someone for free. Most people might have chosen a mate, but I chose Mam. Well, she is my best mate and we'd never really gone on holiday with each other. The flight was horrendous, though. With only a forty-minute stopover in Dubai, we were cooped up inside a metal tube for twenty-four hours travelling to the other side of the universe. It's mad how far south Australia is. And it's massive, too!

Every single day, I was on a flight travelling from city to city. But city to city in Oz takes around six hours. In ten days we went from Sydney to Melbourne, Mackay, Perth, Brisbane, Newcastle and Toowoomba. And in New Zealand, we visited Hamilton and Auckland. The great thing about it was that the weather was topsy turvy, too, which meant we left a windy, cold, rainy Newcastle and arrived in a boiling hot Sydney. Weird!

What I hadn't clocked is that *Geordie Shore* is huge in Australia and when we pitched up at every airport there were fans waiting for autographs. It was so bizarre. I could not have been further away from home and yet people knew who I was! Mam thought it was hilarious that every time we landed this little entourage came to greet us.

Because I was doing PAs every night, we spent most of the days hungover – even Mam! I had set some conditions, though. If I wanted to neck on with anyone during the trip, then she had to skedaddle back to the hotel. I couldn't have Mam around cramping my style, could I? And on a couple of occasions I did end up sending her home. One night early on, I met this mint lad called Zak who I wanted to kiss.

'Mam, I can't kiss a boy in front of you. It's too odd. You're going to have to leave!'

'But, Marnie, I'm having a good time.'

'No, no. Mam, I don't think you understand. It's time to go!'

I was so cruel to her! Another time she had to go was when we were in this really cool bar in Mackay on the east coast. I'd just done a PA at a nearby club and these two lesbians started coming on to me, and because I was mortal, I was bare-faced encouraging them. At one point, Mam even thought one of them was coming on to her!

'I can't take anymore. I'm going back to the hotel,' she said. But I stayed out and ended up tagging along with the lesbians to a gay club. I had no money, and by four a.m. when I left the club, I had no clue how to find my way back to the hotel. Thankfully, a taxi driver took me to the bar where I'd done the PA and the organisers paid the cab driver and took me home. But when I got there, Mam was so flat out from all the wine she'd drunk that she didn't wake up when the buzzer sounded. She was on the fifteenth floor so I was outside screaming up at the top of my lungs . . . but she still didn't wake up. Just as the promoters – who I didn't even know – were offering me a room in the middle of nowhere, she answered. Praise the fucking lord! I've never been so happy to lie down in my life. Australia was a trip that I don't think either of us will forget in a hurry.

I wasn't due back in Newcastle to film for series thirteen until June and July 2016. And after being away in Australia, I was so looking forward to it because another trip abroad was on the cards. It was going to be shot in places like Ayia Napa, Corfu, Ibiza and Magaluf. More weeks of sun and fun. Bring it on! One big decision I'd made was to tell all the girls in the house that I'd come out as bisexual. I'd already told Mam, but I think she knew anyway. Oh, and I'd already done an interview for *Heat* magazine saying as much, so I can't imagine it was a surprise.

Obviously once we got to Magaluf, I was breaking the news for the benefit of the cameras. To be fair, I'd spent a lot of the previous series necking on with Chloe. But what eventually made me want to come out was an experience I'd had earlier that year with an old friend called Nathalie. Nathalie's a full-blown lesbian but it was me who initiated it. We'd been out one night and one thing led to another . . . and something sort of happened. We began necking on in the club, and carried on in the cab and then back at her place. I'd always kissed mates but this was much more than that – it was full-on sex. Even now, I don't feel weird about it and I definitely don't feel ashamed of it. In fact, I would have come out before, but I guess I wasn't sure myself. Now, I am 100 per cent sure. And when people ask me what it's like to have sex with a girl, I say it's amazing. There's no cock involved but all that means is you use your imagination! I hope that me coming out has helped others come out too.

There's nothing worse than not being able to express yourself.

It's not only Mam who's funny about it, though. Some other people in my family are, too, so I did feel a bit anxious at first. As I said before, she finds it hard to understand the 'girl thing'. And when it comes to Nathalie she puts her foot down. 'That lesbian's not coming over tonight!' she always jokes. Even though Nathalie and I are close, Mam always sends her home. Don't get me wrong, she loves Nathalie to bits but whenever she's round, Mam takes her aside, wags her finger and says, 'Nah, nah, nah! You're not getting into my daughter's fanny!' I think she's scared that Nathalie and I could end up going out together forever! She's so embarrassing!

I was also worried about telling Aaron. Since we'd got it together, our relationship had been so on and off. Things were complicated enough without me dumping that on him. Aaron held back his feelings for me *all the time*. I needed him to prove himself to me, but that hadn't happened so far. I always wanted more from Aaron, but for some reason he couldn't give it. For example, just before I went to Australia, I went out with *Ex on the Beach* star Jordan Davies – who I'd met through Chloe Goodman – on Valentine's Day. All the papers reported it as me standing Aaron up on Valentine's Day, but that couldn't have been further from the truth. I'd got bored waiting for Aaron to ask me out, but he never did. 'If you're not going to take me out on the most special day of the year, then I'll go out with someone else,' I told him. And his reply? 'Fine.' But Aaron wasn't fine. I'd called his bluff and he was fuming! He was the one that told the papers about me and Jordan. How low is that?

It didn't take long for me to find out how Aaron felt about the 'girl thing', either. On our first night filming for *Geordie Shore* in Magaluf, Chloe and I couldn't stop dancing in this club. But it wasn't just dancing – Chloe was full-on kissing my foof! In front of everyone! Aaron was foaming. Maybe sheer jealousy prompted him to ask me to be his girlfriend. Naturally, I was dead chuffed. I wanted to be Aaron's girlfriend. Deep down, did I think me and Aaron would last? It took the biggest opportunity of my life to find out.

CHAPTER 19

LIVE FROM THE BIG BROTHER HOUSE

From when I was a kid I'd dreamed of going on *Big Brother*, but never in a million years did I think I'd actually be asked. And I *never ever* imagined it would be the celebrity version. Again, it was all down to my agent Craig.

Just before filming series thirteen, the producers asked to meet me. We'd already had an introductory chat, but I wasn't hopeful. Although others in the *Geordie Shore* house had been on *Big Brother*, I knew I'd never be one of the favourites. I mean, the public *love* Charlotte, who won in 2013, because she's a complete howl, even though at the time I hated her and couldn't understand why anyone voted for her. And Scott, who won in 2016 – well, Scott's just

Scott. Despite our ups and downs, Scott's lovely. Although he is a nightmare to live with. Because he has severe OCD, he's the only one who uses the washing machine in *Geordie Shore*. And if he's cooking, he won't let anyone near him. Once he had a radgie with me over a pair of socks I'd stolen from him – he's that bad!

Anyway, I was doing a shoot in Manchester for a sports clothing range I'd put together with ForeverModo when the producers called Craig. They'd finalised the line-up, but someone had fallen through.

'*Big Brother*'s on the line. They want you in London tomorrow.'

'Are you fucking kidding me?'

I thought Craig was taking the piss! But, no. When I rocked up at Gilgamesh in Camden, which is this posh restaurant, two producers from the production company were waiting for me. It was hardly an interview, though. 'Just be yourself,' I thought. So I got mortal and chatted non-stop for two hours! Just like the commissioners on *Geordie Shore,* I gelled with them immediately. 'What's the craziest thing you've done in the house?' Mmmm. That was a hard one, but hiding the dishes from Vicky sprung to mind immediately! Hopefully I'd done enough to convince them, but nothing was confirmed until I was on a beach in Ayia Napa in the middle of filming. We were on a three-day break and Craig was the first person to ring me. Knowing that two days after the end of filming *Geordie Shore*, I'd be in another house with strangers was totally surreal! But I wouldn't let myself get too excited about it. Knowing my luck, it could all fall through at the last minute.

First, though, I had the Aaron situation to deal with. Did I go into *Big Brother* attached? As far as I was concerned, Aaron had done nothing to make me want to be with him. I don't know where I got the strength from, but the minute we finished filming, I got into his car with him and told him I was going into the house single.

'Well, fucking get out the car.'

Can you believe that was his first reaction? But I stubbornly stayed put and talked, and he understood. Had he acted like a proper boyfriend, I may have felt differently. I waited so long for Aaron, and he'd turned out to be one massive disappointment. Anyway, I reckon if the tables had been turned, he'd have done the same.

Two nights before, I stayed in a hotel in London. I was a mixture of nerves and excitement and I was so bored of waiting I dyed my hair. Big mistake! The colour was far too dark so I had to get a hairdresser to come over and bleach it out. But the bleach made it go bright orange. Fuck! Eventually, she got it to a medium brown colour but what people don't know is that for the whole four weeks I was in *Big Brother* I didn't wash my hair once. Every time I splashed in the pool or got a soaking I noticed dye dripping out exposing the orange underneath. I couldn't risk looking like Coco the Clown. It was mingin'!

Entering *Big Brother* felt so different to entering *Geordie Shore.* First of all, it's a show with a public vote and that's terrifying. If *Geordie Shore* had been a competition, I'm sure I would have been booted off ages ago! Before I entered I went into hiding. There's no TV and no phone, but I snuck out for a few drinks. What a relief! When I did finally leave the hotel, I'd had seven double vodkas. Woohoo! I was flying. Then I was blindfolded and driven to a set of double doors and left there.

'As soon as those doors open, walk out.'

My chaperone left. Suddenly, it was just me on my own shitting myself. Through the door, I could faintly hear my introduction video running and the crowd cheering.

'I'm Marnie. I've got the best-looking vagina in Newcastle!'

Why the fuck did I let them record that? In a few seconds, I had to go out and face the crowd! I loved the black hot pants and thigh-length boots I had on but I couldn't help feeling so self-conscious about my disaster hair.

Surprisingly, I got an amazing reception and Emma Willis was so bubbly that she made me forget my nerves instantly. We'd never met, but I got such good vibes from her and she is stunningly beautiful – far prettier than she looks on TV. Immediately she asked me whether I'd win like Scott and Charlotte. Er . . . no pressure! 'I'll definitely break the rules,' I announced.

Fear didn't hit me until I was walking down the stairs. I thought, 'I've watched this for so many years and now it's me!' It felt so disorientating, my head was spinning!

Already in the house when I arrived were TV presenters Christopher Biggins and Saira Khan, who I got awful vibes from straight away. Then there was American actor Frankie Grande and the guy off *EastEnders*, Ricky Norwood. Also welcoming me was Renee Graziano – she was wild and talked proper New York, so she put 'motherfucker' into every sentence. Turns out she is a gangster's wife who starred in the US reality show *Mob Wives*. Still to come was the DJ James Whale, who I'd never heard of. Same with singer Aubrey O'Day. Then there was *X Factor* contestant Katie Waissel; Anthea Turner's ex, Grant Bovey; glamour models Chloe Khan and Samantha Fox; rapper Heavy D; *Ex on the Beach* star Stephen Bear; and *TOWIE* star Lewis Bloor.

Hilariously, I'd only met Lewis before, and that was only briefly at a party a year before. But the weird thing was, I'd seen his willy countless times! My agent Craig was Lewis's agent at the time and for some reason, don't ask me how, Craig had this picture of Lewis's cock on his phone. Every time I was feeling sad, he'd flash it up on-screen. 'But Marnie . . .' he'd grin, and we'd both stare dreamily at it!

Other than the gold decor and being amazed at how small the house is in reality, the only other thing that jumped out at me was Frankie. He was so fun, hyper and lovable. I thought he was mortal like me, but later I found out he doesn't even drink! Then it struck me. This isn't an hour of TV for me to watch; I'm living with these people twenty-four hours a day. I'd heard that loads of the celebrities have weird and wonderful demands written into their contract, but I only had one: that I could take my vibrator in with me. It's shaped like an ice cream cone. They were probably thinking, who asks for that? But I reckoned I'd get very bored and lonely!

I found the first night very awkward. At first I was trying to be friendly and happy and I wanted to get to know everyone, but Saira cornered me and started proper grilling me about how much I earned. She wanted to know all the details of my bank balance and what I got paid to go on *Geordie Shore*. And she wanted to know why I had sex on TV. To be honest, I felt very intimidated by her. I'd seen her on *Loose Women* so I knew she was very opinionated, but it felt like she was judging me *all the time*. Even Mam doesn't do that! I thought, 'I've come here to be myself and here you are with your patronising, snooty attitude.' She spent the whole time trying to embarrass me. So to make her feel as uncomfortable I asked her, 'Who are you going to have sex with in the house?' I even asked her if she masturbated, and buzzed my vibrator on her knee as a joke. Unfortunately, me going out of my way to shock her was the only footage the public saw and the rest of the conversation wasn't aired. Later, I did flash my boobs at her, but it was only to lighten the atmosphere – you could have cut it with a knife. In *Geordie Shore*, no one would have blinked twice at the sight of my boobs, but I was realising this was a different house.

Saira couldn't take a joke at all. When she got evicted and said publicly that I was no better than a prostitute, it did affect me. Most of all, I felt sad because after that first night, I made an effort to get to know her and told her lots of very personal things about myself, yet she still went out and slagged me off. It was like she'd formed this opinion of me from the off. I was the youngest girl in the house and young people like to have fun. What I learned about Saira during our time together was that she had no self-awareness and I don't think she ever thought of herself as a difficult person. It was the same with Heavy D. He didn't talk. He just grunted, and I found him hard to fathom. He was always trying to wind up the house, but most of the time it didn't work; it was just annoying.

The weird thing was that although I did end up having sex with Lewis on the programme, it had never been my game plan. Beforehand, I reckoned getting with someone would disadvantage me. I wanted people to see me. But Lewis and I naturally gravitated towards each other. Of all the people there, I liked him straight away. When I'd met him a year previous he'd been drunk and a bit weird. Lewis gets dead fidgety when he's pissed, so I don't remember talking to him much. But when he walked into the *Big Brother* house he was completely sober and shaking like a leaf. I thought, 'This big six-foot boy looks like a model. He's manly but nervous too.' It was so cute.

On the first morning, I had such a hangover and I was in bed with Renee! I have no idea how that happened. Early in the morning she was shouting, 'I'm so motherfucking jet lagged!' How come I picked the scariest woman in the house to sleep with? If I'm honest, it took me ages to adjust. I was used to waking up with all my *Geordie Shore* mates, but in *Big Brother* I opened my eyes to this random collection of older people. I was way out of my comfort zone. Thankfully, I'd taken in a picture of me and Sophie to keep me sane.

I had to love Lewis because the first thing he did was make me breakfast. I was that hungover, I thought

I was going to spew eating it. To please him, I forced down this gorgeous, colourful plate of organic egg, avocado and grilled bacon. I was so mortified, though, because Aubrey kept whispering *very* loudly in my ear about Lewis, '*Someone* wants some pussy!'

Lewis covered the fact that he fancied me because he offered breakfast to everyone, but I had this funny feeling he only wanted to cook for me. In fact, Lewis made me breakfast every day. From the off, he had my back. How romantic is that?

I don't know whether it's because we were all on reality shows, but from the start me, Lewis and Bear stuck together like a wolf pack. The boys weren't half as bitchy as the girls had first been in *Geordie Shore.* And with Lewis and Bear I didn't have to force any small talk. Bear was so gobby and I found him a hoot. That boy made me laugh so much. Having said that, he did go out with Vicky Pattison so I was a bit apprehensive about him at first.

If I'm brutally honest, I found both Bear and Lewis sexy, but after around four days, Lewis had the edge. He had this groomed look and a serious side that I found very attractive. Whenever I looked at Bear, I thought, 'Fling.' But I didn't want that. If I was looking for anyone it was a potential boyfriend – the sort of person I could introduce to me nana. I realise now that Lewis didn't show all of his personality in the *Big Brother* house. He can be dead fiery and he doesn't put up with any shit and that's a turn on for me. But I also know there's a whole other side to him, too – a cheating, devious side. More of that later . . . But in *Big Brother*, Lewis was adorable.

What I also loved about being in the house was that we were left alone. Obviously we could go to the diary room whenever we wanted, but I cannot tell you the number of times I rang on the bell! Embarrassingly, I plucked up the courage early on to tell *Big Brother* I had thrush and needed a doctor. I'd been taking antibiotics, but they hadn't worked and, no joke, my fanny was so itchy. What a nightmare! Despite what Saira might have thought, I couldn't have had sex with anyone when I entered that house even if I'd wanted to! Anyway, thank God they gave me suppositories that got to work quickly.

What I found the most bizarre was the drama that the Americans created over absolutely nothing. And I mean *absolutely nothing*. For example, if a drop of coffee was spilled they'd shout, '*Oh my God!* There's starving children in Africa and you've spilled the coffee!' 'Chill out,' I thought. 'That would never happen in the *Geordie Shore* house!' Then later on, they found a pair of my knickers on the floor that I'd mistakenly brought with me because I'd packed so quickly. Of course it had to be a pair that me dog Elvis had chewed the crotch right out of. '*Oh my God! Whose fucking animal ate the crotch?*' They wouldn't shut up about the knickers and they even started throwing them around the bedroom. Poor Bear – at one point they were throwing them in his face. I was mortified! They all blamed the crotchless knickers on Chloe Khan, who'd been evicted by that point, so I let them go on thinking that until one day I felt so guilty I had to fess up that they were mine. We giggled for days and the Elvis-chewed pants became a running joke in the house.

Thank God for the tasks, because otherwise I would have been *really* bored. On day three we had to participate in a task called 'Game of Phones' where we were given facts about each of the housemates. We had to guess which fact belonged to which housemate and each team had to stand in a phone box assigned to that person. I'd watched the tasks for so long that all I kept thinking was, 'I'm actually doing a task!' I was buzzing! And it was fun because we learned that Biggins posed naked for a photoshoot with an octopus, Bear slept with his mate's cousin, and Aubrey froze her dog's sperm!

If we didn't match the right fact to the right person we got covered with thick, pink and green, sloppy gunge inside the phone box, which I would have loved had it not been for my disastrous hair-dye problem.

My hair was exactly the reason I didn't mind some of the punishments either. For example, early on we had our hot water and electricity switched off because Saira, Bear, Biggins, James and Renee were caught discussing nominations. 'Well, it's not like I'm going to wash anyway!' I thought. But the others were so dramatic about it!

One task I absolutely loved was the talent show hosted by Biggins called *Big Brother's Big Show Off*. Aubrey, Frankie and Renee were judges and we all had to get up and do a turn. Grant read out a motivational presentation about self-belief, which was really boring. Then Chloe Kahn had to be a calendar girl for every month of the year, which almost made me wet myself. Then it came to my turn and I had to star as a pregnant girlfriend caught in a love triangle between Bear and Lewis. The minute I learned what I had to do, I thought it was very clever of the programme's producers. They'd clearly been watching the three of us as a group, always huddled together. Sam Fox sang her hit 'Touch Me' and got the most votes and won. She was a really good performer, but I didn't bond with Sam in the house; I don't know why.

It was obvious who was desperate to win from early on. The Americans were so competitive and I reckoned Frankie and Aubrey were playing a game all the time. Aubrey was going out of her way to be nice to everybody and she was always starting deep and meaningful conversations with people. Frankie was so over-the-top and I felt he was trying too hard. Although I had no expectation of winning, I was keen not to be the first person to be evicted. I actually had sleepless nights about it because it would have been gutting having to face the crowd knowing the public didn't want you in there. I wasn't sad when Grant and James were the first to be nominated for eviction, but I was surprised Grant was the first to go. I liked him. I think he fancied me, though. He was this very attractive older man and I would wind him up with comments like, 'I think you and I will spoon!' That's just my sense of humour, but I reckon he actually believed he was in with a chance! It was a shame he left, and although I enjoyed James's company, the age gap meant we didn't have much in common.

I wasn't upset in the slightest when Biggins was forced to leave. He was removed for offensive comments, but thank God I wasn't around to hear them. He slagged off bisexuals and said they were to blame for the AIDS virus. Had I been there, I wouldn't have been able to keep my trap shut. Then he made an anti-Jewish comment in front of Katie Waissel, who is Jewish. When we were told he wasn't coming back, I thought, 'Great! One less person in the house.' I'd not really bonded with Biggins and I found him loud and overbearing. Everyone found Heavy D hard work, too. He was a miserable, old fat man and it was no shock that Lewis hated being around him. At one point, Lewis even threw a drink over him and got separated off into another house. Bear, on the other hand, was on a mission to irritate *everyone*, but he did it in such a loveable way. Fortunately, I was never on the receiving end of any of it so I found it entertaining.

Everything came to a head in the task 'Don't Burst My Bubble' when we had to wear these humongous balloons on our chests to protect at all costs. The people whose balloons didn't get popped got to celebrate at a party. But there was a twist: it was a secret mission that Big Brother had got Saira and I to do. Of course, I burst Lewis's bubble first as I wanted him at the party but I had to pretend it was an accident. I was gutted! But Bear burst Katie's on purpose and, after that, the whole house exploded. She stormed out in tears calling him a 'fucking dick'. Then he burst mine after I burst his, and that was followed by an almighty argument between Renee and Bear. To avoid Bear bursting their balloons, Frankie, Aubrey, Renee and Chloe locked themselves in another room, but Bear kept winding them up by shouting through the door.

'You're acting like an asshole. I can't do this anymore, I don't have patience for this,' Renee screamed. Then, after Bear popped Ricky Norwood's balloon, he started shouting too. 'Don't say my name, you ugly motherfucker. You've got no mates, so fuck off. You're an ugly human being.' Oh my God! They took it all so seriously and I thought it was all going to kick off. It was worse than *Geordie Shore*!

Thank God I had my little refuge in Lewis. We actually kissed in the store cupboard on the fourth day, but it was only a peck when we were fetching gin and tonic. I thought, 'Marnie, you're such a love-sick puppy you'll find love wherever you go!' But I couldn't ignore the butterflies in my stomach whenever I was near him. And we shared a bed from early on, but I swear it was only spooning. There's nothing to do in that house other than smoke and kiss, so Lewis and I ended up kissing loads in the first two weeks. Wherever anyone turned Lewis and I were stuck to each other kissing. I actually felt drunk on love.

Surprisingly, the first time we had sex was more than two weeks in, but it was never shown. It was on a night when I was up for eviction and I was so terrified, I got palatic. Bizarrely, Lewis and I had actually fallen out earlier in the evening because he hadn't chosen to save me in a task called 'Selfish or Selfless'. In the game you had to choose to play for the house or for yourself. Lewis chose to play for the house, but this meant he wasn't on my team. I was furious! 'Why isn't he supporting me?' I thought.

There was no way I could stay mad at Lewis for long, though, and later that evening we ended up having sex in the bedroom toilet. Even though the toilet stank and it was so cramped it was still really romantic. In fact it was so funny and it was exciting.

Afterwards I was called into the diary room. I learned that Big Brother always calls you in after you have sex with someone just to make sure it's not against your will.

'Are you OK with everything that's happened, Marnie?'

'Yeah, course.'

'Did you want any of that to happen?'

'Jeeezzz, I started it!'

The whole time I was talking to Big Brother I couldn't get Lewis out of my mind.

The second time we had sex was in the shower, and Lewis was so sweet. The showers had these bright spotlights in them and I became so self-conscious about all the scarring around my boobs that I kept holding them to hide it. But Lewis made me feel dead confident about my body. 'Phoaaaar.' He made these funny noises whenever he looked at me. When he was washing his hair I couldn't help but spy on his willy. I couldn't get over how big it was – I was gobsmacked. When we had sex in the shower, it was so romantic – the shower had some lovely sparkly lights and it was super cute. I knew I was in serious trouble with him because I'd never felt so in love before and those feelings were super strong.

After that we were so into each other that we were

inseparable. He even had his willy inside me one afternoon when we were spooning in bed. We weren't actually having sex, but no one knew. Renee was wandering around the room talking about what pasta she was going to cook for tea and a couple of the others were milling around tidying up. We couldn't stop giggling – it was our big secret!

It's why, when Lewis eventually got evicted three weeks in I was devastated. He'd been my best friend in that house. I've never watched Lewis's eviction back, but I know I was so embarrassing. I bawled my eyes out for hours. People couldn't understand it, and kept asking, 'Why are you crying?' It felt like someone was ripping my heart out. Lewis had been my support system, and because the house is like being in another universe, when someone leaves, it's as if they're going back to earth. It feels so distant. I had such a depression session and I lay in bed and sniffed his bandana all night. Pathetic or what? Once he'd gone, I was desperate to be evicted. I didn't expect to be in the final, and part of me wished I hadn't been. The days after Lewis left just dragged and dragged and dragged.

All along I'd been convinced that Bear would win. He is such a character and although nobody has any clue what the public are thinking when you're in the house, I hoped people wanted him to win. For me, he made the show. I had no idea what the public thought of me either and I'd be lying if I said I didn't worry about that. All I hoped was that I'd done enough for people to think I was an OK person and maybe they'd seen a different side to me than in *Geordie Shore*.

By the end of the series, I'd survived three evictions, Lewis leaving, and the sheer boredom of the house. Walking down those stairs to greet Emma not long after I came fourth was the weirdest feeling ever. I felt like this mole emerging from deep underground. Don't ask me what I said in my exit interview because I've no idea – all I remember is telling Emma that I'd only taken in four days' worth of clothes because I didn't expect to be there for long. But the crowd gave me this massive cheer and that felt brilliant. Seeing Lewis flash up on the big screen waiting for me backstage was also truly amazing. I couldn't wait to hug him, kiss him again.

CHAPTER 20

BLOORY EYED

If it hadn't been for Lewis, coming out of *Big Brother* would have been a total come down. Instead, it was brilliant. That night after the wrap party we stayed with each other in the Village Hotel and had sex properly. Unlike being in the house where you were constantly looking over your shoulder wondering whether the cameras were filming you, we could just enjoy ourselves. Since Aaron, I'd closed myself off to feeling loved up with someone, but Lewis brought out my soft side again. He was so gentlemanly and protective that I felt I could let go.

The following day, reality sank in. Immediately, I had to do *The Wright Stuff* and then fly to Ireland for a PA. That was followed a day or so later by an appearance on *This Morning*. I'd not done much live TV before and it was pretty nerve-wracking. But I don't lie and when I was on the sofa with Ruth and Eamonn, I did admit that I'd been disappointed that Saira Khan had slagged me off after the show. Funnily, she'd walked up to me at the wrap party and said, 'Marnie, there's been a bit of press since I've been out, but don't believe everything you hear.' But I went on YouTube and saw exactly what she'd said about me being no better than a prostitute when she appeared on *The Wright Stuff*, so from then on I knew she was a fake.

That week I also realised it was going to be more difficult than I'd expected to spend time with Lewis. We both had hectic schedules. He'd been doing loads of personal training since he stopped appearing in *TOWIE*, and he'd been working hard to get his fitness business off the ground. I think Lewis would be the first to admit that TV wasn't really for him. He hated all the storylines and being told what and what not to say. He's always said he never felt like he could be himself on reality TV.

Following *Big Brother*, I was desperate to see Mam but the minute I was up in Newcastle, Lewis didn't contact me at all. The silence was really upsetting. I was starting to see a whole different side to him that hadn't been obvious in the house. Occasionally he'd reply to my texts but his behaviour wasn't half as full-on. I thought, 'What have I done? Why don't you like me anymore?' Later I learned that Lewis had some personal shit going on that wouldn't be fair for me to talk about. Anyway, it took him a long time to be open with me about his life. I practically had to beg him and, in the early stages of our relationship, I even debated dumping him because suddenly all he wanted to do was get fucked up with his mates and go off to music festivals.

The turning point came just before we booked a holiday to Barcelona.

'I can't be with you if you're going to be like this, Lewis.'

'Babe, I really want to be with you.'

'Well, you need to show it.'

For the first time in a long time, I felt in control of myself. I wasn't going to put up with any crap. Of course, now I know Lewis was a cheating arsehole in Barcelona, but that long weekend away was dead romantic. The minute we landed we set off exploring the city and we got a personal tour guide to take us around. Then we ate out in these gorgeous tapas bars and sunbathed on the beach. I loved it. There was also a huge festival going on in the city, so we milled around and watched all the entertainment. All the time it felt like Lewis and I were reconnecting. We couldn't walk down the street without holding hands or kissing.

We only had one major argument in Barcelona. It was ridiculous and it was over a boy called Kyle Walker. Kyle was someone I'd known from Newcastle. I'd kissed him before, but that was years ago and we'd always been just friends. While we were eating out at a restaurant, I noticed on his Twitter feed that Kyle was in Barcelona. How spooky was that?

'Oh my God, Kyle Walker's in Barcelona!' I blurted out. Immediately Lewis was on the defensive.

'Have you kissed him?'

'Yeah, yeah, yeah but it was years ago. It's not like that – we're just friends.'

'I want to meet him.'

'Why?'

'Tell him we'll meet him and we'll have a drink . . .'

The last thing I wanted to do was have a drink with Kyle, especially as Lewis was acting so jealous. Kyle is good-looking and I knew Lewis would jump to conclusions. But Lewis was forceful and we did end up meeting Kyle. We all got on, and I hoped Lewis would see there was nothing between us, but on the way back to the hotel, he kept banging on about the way I'd been looking at Kyle and how I still fancied him. Then Kyle rang me on my mobile, only I had him saved in my addresses as 'My Boo'. I can't have changed from when Kyle and I had a thing going. Shit! Lewis was furious.

'*My Boo?*'

'Lewis, I'm with you. There's nothing going on!'

No matter how much pleading I did with Lewis, I sensed he didn't believe me. He'd turned into this green-eyed monster. But Lewis was hardly a saint himself. I think part of Lewis's problem was that he hadn't been in a proper relationship before me and he found it hard to adjust. Being faithful to one person was definitely not Lewis's history with girls. Until I came along, he'd never considered settling down. He said as much when he appeared on *Loose Women* while I was still in the *Big Brother* house. Hearing him say that had made me feel really secure, but now I wasn't so sure . . .

Despite a few hiccups in the months after Barcelona, we did end up doing loads of nice things together. For example, we went to the theatre to see the musical *Motown*, and Lewis took me out for loads of nice meals when I was in London. The distance was hard, though, and when I was back in Newcastle, I did finish with him briefly. Looking back, I was probably overly dramatic, but he'd gone for a night out with his mates in London and I couldn't get hold of him. He didn't text me till five p.m. the next day. I thought, 'Fuck you!' In a rage I deleted all his pictures off my Instagram page. No one could accuse me of doing things by halves! When I'm angry, I'm very impulsive. But Lewis did the big, 'I'm sorry, babe,' number and he won me round. We even took another holiday together in Ibiza. That was amazing – just sea, sand and partying and each other for company. It really felt as though we were a proper couple on that trip.

In October I was due to go back into the *Geordie Shore* house to film series fourteen. I knew that would be a test for Lewis because Aaron would be there . . . and Gary. And, as I've said before, being in the show affects your relationships on the outside. Plus, since Ibiza, Lewis and I had talked about me moving down to London full-time and getting a place together. This time, I couldn't blag it. I was entering the house with a serious boyfriend, and it was a boyfriend I *really* wanted to be with, despite Lewis's often weird behaviour.

I won't lie, Lewis can be such a peculiar person. Even Mam says he's unique. He can be very impatient, but he can be very spiritual, too. He's the sort of person that if the sun is shining, he'll take it as a sign that something good is happening within him. I thought I was bad, but Lewis can get really deep! He reads loads of self-help books and he can beat himself up a lot. For example, if he has a lie-in after a big night out, he gets properly stressed. He says he feels worthless. But I'm completely the opposite. I think, 'Chill out, Lewis! I'm going to watch crappy films *all day* and nurse my hangover from under the duvet! And eat a massive Happy Meal!' Anyway, with Lewis,

I knew that if he saw me mortal or necking on it would really affect him.

All that pressure got to me after the first week of filming. I hadn't banked on how much I'd miss him. I was like a wounded animal, moping around and feeling sorry for myself. It's definitely one of the reasons I had an epic meltdown one night when we were filming in the Riverside in Newcastle.

Hands up, I was palatic, but I'd also had enough. As usual when we are filming in the club there's loads of security around, and there's always an area cordoned-off where we hang out. Most of the time people are nosy and just want to watch the filming, but on this occasion the crowd were throwing drinks and plastic tumblers up on to the balcony and jeering at us. It was horrible. There's loads more security around us now than when I started in the programme. They couldn't control these people and I ended up having the contents of an ice bucket tipped across me. That was the last straw and I snapped. I thought, 'These people don't realise how hard filming is!' Without my phone or any contact with Lewis I just wanted out of there. I was desperate to go home.

Of course, all the newspapers ran that story of me bawling my eyes out, not wearing shoes, looking mortal and having to be talked down by the crew, but I don't apologise for it. That night, I really had had enough.

While series fourteen was fun, it did feel like the programme had changed. Holly had announced she wasn't coming back in the break and Charlotte had also quit the show. Sadly, she'd had a bit of a drama with Gaz and had suffered an ectopic pregnancy and didn't feel she could return. Considering how long it took me to bond with them, I missed them like crazy. Now there were all these randoms parachuted in which made up fourteen house members. Brilliantly, I still had Chloe, Scott, Gaz, Aaron, Nathan, Sophie, who came back for good, and a guy called Marty who'd joined in series twelve. As I write, the new series hasn't yet aired, but you'll be introduced to Zahida, Chelsea, Sam, Sarah, Abbie, Electra, Billy and Eve. It will be interesting to see how they are received. For me, though, what makes *Geordie Shore* so much fun is that the storylines centre on a handful of characters who the fans fall in love with. With loads of random people, I don't know if the viewers will feel the same.

Being away from Lewis definitely put a strain on our relationship but, Lewis being Lewis, he didn't tell me how he felt. Instead of being honest, he bottled everything up and the minute I came out of the house he became very distant and wanted to hang out with his mates all the time. I thought, 'One minute you're serious about us and the next you don't give a toss!' It was very confusing.

To make the situation better, we agreed to start looking for a flat in London straight away. If we were living together then the distance wouldn't be a problem. I can't say I wasn't apprehensive. It was the first time I'd lived away from home and London is a big place when you don't know anyone. Part of me wanted to be with my own mates and not have to rely on Lewis's friends and family for company. Having said that, I loved Lewis's mum from the off. She's a very strong lady and very caring. I soon realised that she would do anything for us. Of course, that reassured Mam, who is desperate for me to come home. If she had her way, I'd buy a house in Newcastle and Mam, Eric and me would all live in it together forever!

What was lovely was that we all got to spend Christmas together, like a proper big family. Lewis's mam, my mam, Eric and Lewis, and I had such a relaxed time. Lewis's mam lives nearby and his auntie's, where we spent Christmas Day, is in deepest darkest Essex where it's just fields and farms. It's so different to the bustle of inner city London. Our flat, too, was way out east but not too far away – perfect for travelling into a place called Stratford where there's a massive shopping mall, and handy for my work meetings in central London.

After the high of Christmas, Lewis suddenly went back to being really moody and distant. Me moving down hadn't helped at all, and I felt like we were back to square one almost overnight. I loved Lewis, but being with him wasn't working and I had to face facts. The worse things got, the more it felt like Lewis was taking his issues out on me. Sometimes I didn't even feel like I was his girlfriend; as if we weren't part of a team at all.

'I'm going to go home. It's not working,' I said to him a couple of days before New Year.

Lewis was very silent. We didn't even row. Instead he said he was going out, and I agreed to pack up my stuff and wait till he got back.

Packing didn't take long seeing as I'd only brought a suitcase and a few bits, and I was just about to get in the car when Lewis reappeared. He looked terrible. I was sad to be leaving him, but in my heart I knew it was for the best. For that whole journey home, I felt so miserable – there was this empty feeling inside me. What made it worse was that my phone kept buzzing with messages from Lewis begging me to come back. He'd never begged me like that before, so there was a part of me that thought maybe he could change. He was so confusing. One minute, he was full-on with me and the next he was pushing me away.

All I needed was to get my head together and have a night out with my girls. Luckily, Charlotte, Sophie and Chloe were all home for New Year and that was very special. I'm so lucky to have such great mates around me. First off, we stayed locally for a few drinks and some food then went on to a party at Charlotte's. It was such a fun night. I even tweeted that I was bringing in the New Year single, but that was partly because I wanted Lewis to know that he couldn't keep manipulating me. Bizarrely, the next morning I woke up to even more texts from him. 'Can we give it another go?' 'Please come home, babe.' My head was spinning. As complex as Lewis was, I did have faith in him. I believed we could be as happy as we wanted to be. Call me stupid, but I agreed to give it one more go.

In January and February, I didn't regret making that decision at all. When I came back to London it felt like the air had been cleared and we were starting afresh. He was a different person and we began to love spending time with each other. One day we even realised that we hadn't left each other's side for four whole weeks, as if we were Siamese twins or something.

'We're in a really good place,' I kept saying to him, as if I couldn't even believe it myself. We even talked about getting a nicer place together a bit further out near the Essex countryside. And I was so proud to have Lewis on my arm at the NTA Awards in January, although everyone went a bit mental over my dress. I never wear any underwear normally. I can't be bothered. I had this beautiful, black lace see-through dress on but I did try it on in front of Lewis beforehand to check just how see-through it was. Promise! Believe it or not, I would never choose to go out with my fanny on show.

'Nah, babe. Can't see anything. You look amazing,' Lewis said and, anyway, that dress would have been ruined with knickers on underneath. What I hadn't anticipated was all the flashes from the hundreds of cameras lined up on the red carpet. It meant that in the official shots from the night you could see my foof. Thank God I'd shaved! Of course, the papers were really mean, calling it a fashion fail and a wardrobe malfunction. Cue Twitter, which went nuts. One person even posted that I should be done for public indecency! As Mam says, if people are talking about you, it must be good. Honestly, though, when the lights weren't on me, that dress looked amazing and no one commented once on being able to see my vagina.

I've found that when the press get hold of something, they use it to say all sorts of crap about you. It's a part of being in the public eye I've had to get used to, but I don't think I'll ever enjoy it. Before Christmas I even had a story appear about me alongside a film. Apparently, I was taking cocaine in the toilets of a club in Shrewsbury. I even know the girls who took the video because they were acquaintances of Lewis. But I wasn't taking drugs. I was holding the bag for two of the other girls while they had a wee. Unsurprisingly, the papers made me out to be some sort of drug-crazed celebrity. As far as I know those girls didn't even get any money from making that video public. Sometimes, you have to just shrug your shoulders and think, what's the point? If people are going to make stuff up about me, let them. I know what the truth is . . .

CHAPTER 21

HE LOVES ME. HE LOVES ME NOT . . .

Lewis and I were in such a good place there was a part of me that didn't want to spoil it by going back to *Geordie Shore*. In the meantime, I'd started writing this book and we were making so many plans together it was ridiculous. We even found a bigger flat and moved into it towards the end of January. I'm not saying Lewis and I didn't argue – we argued all the time, but it was over really stupid things. For example, once we had this two-hour epic because he accused me of being obsessed with the Kardashians. All I'd done was look at Kim on Instagram and comment about what she was wearing. Suddenly he went into meltdown.

'You love the Kardashians. It's all you ever talk about!' he began shouting.

'No I don't! I just notice what they are wearing.'

'No, Marnie. You *really* love them!'

From the off Lewis knew exactly what buttons to press to get me completely wound up, but I think it's part of the reason I found him so sexy.

Because series fourteen of *Geordie Shore* was being filmed in two parts, I was contracted to go back in February. My bladder was really playing up, though, so instead of staying for the whole duration I ended up filming for two weeks. What a laugh! First off, we went skiing in the Swiss Alps. I thought I'd love the whole skiing thing, but I quickly realised it wasn't for me. It was so cold! For three days we went sledging, skiing, built snowmen, and we went ice skating on an actual lake, which was terrifying. We all got altitude sickness. Poor Sophie – for the first three days she was in such a bad way, it was coming out of both ends! At times, I was so dizzy I forgot I was filming and left the frames when I wasn't supposed to. I think I even forgot my own name in some of the scenes!

I had been looking forward to the après-ski, but the clubs could not have been more different to the ones in Newcastle. For starters, the girls didn't wear make-up and everybody dressed down. On occasion, I saw girls still dressed in their skiwear! You can imagine how we stuck out like sore thumbs? At home, if you don't have your cleavage out, at least two pairs of lashes and killer heels, you're underdressed! The girls were dead stuck up, too, which only made me, Chloe and Sophie want to shock them more.

'It's so embarrassing when girls wear make-up on the slopes!' we overheard them bitching about us.

'Marn, have you got a mirror? I need to put my make-up on!' Sophie started shouting.

Then Chloe started touching her boobs. 'Oh God, this bra is soooooo tight. My boobs are soooooo big.'

We were being dead vulgar and going up and blatantly asking boys for their numbers. Us Geordie girls know how to make our own fun, that's for sure. Anyway, I thought I looked mint with my bright pink luminous lipstick on. It complemented the snow so well!

All the time I was filming, I was missing Lewis, but this time around it felt like we were in the strongest place we'd ever been. He'd made me feel so secure before I left – he'd stopped going out and partying and it was like he'd settled down. At the start of our relationship loads of people on social media had griefed us that it was a showmance because we'd met on *Big Brother*. At times, I questioned it myself. Why are we together? Now, though, I was sure. I loved Lewis and he loved me. He even drove me to Newcastle Airport before my flight to Switzerland. We wanted to be with each other until the last moment. 'It's only two weeks,' I said. I mean, two weeks isn't a long time, is it? As the saying goes, absence makes the heart grow fonder. What could possibly go wrong?

The day I got back from skiing, I was able to ring Lewis. It was amazing to hear his voice. 'I love you and miss you,' he said, and I believed him. Back in Newcastle, all the drama was around the newbies in the house but admittedly, there were things I did that I knew Lewis would not be happy about. For example, there was one night when I got so palatic I passed out in the club and had to be carried into a taxi. Aaron ended up giving me a fireman's lift all the way to bed. Another night, I poured a drink over Aaron's head but I don't even remember why. I just did it! Him and I started having this pretend fight and, although it was all very innocent, I had a funny feeling Lewis would take it the wrong way. What Lewis doesn't understand is that I have known Aaron for years, and I do feel close to certain people in the house. It doesn't automatically mean I'm having sex with them! I don't think Aaron and I should have ever got together as boyfriend and girlfriend now. We're much happier being mates.

Then, back in Newcastle, Sophie, Chloe and I hit an all-time low. One of the biggest problems in the house is that the toilet is so far from the girls' bedroom. Most of the time we can't even be bothered going for a wee. This one night, we were all so drunk we wrapped up a towel and lay it in the middle of the room. I weed on it first, then Sophie followed, then Chloe followed after that. Then I went back to be sick on it and one of the new girls, Sarah, also threw up on it shortly afterwards. I know, I know – it's gross! The most amazing thing was, when I picked up the towel the next day, not one dribble of sick or wee had touched the floor. We may have been pissed, but we knew how to aim!

'Marnie, I'm twenty-seven and I'm weeing into a towel. It has to stop!' Sophie moaned to me the next day, but a couple of nights later, when she wasn't even as drunk, she did exactly the same!

One of the most difficult parts of being away was that I wasn't going to be with Lewis for Valentine's Day. I felt so deflated. A few days before, on one of our down days, I did have time to run out and buy him a card and I asked the crew to send it for us. Inside the message was dead soppy. 'I love you so much and I can't wait to get back to you and our beautiful home. We're going to spend 100 more Valentine's Days together.' It was three pages long – practically an essay!

On the actual day, I pleaded with the crew to let me ring Lewis, but they refused saying I'd have to wait until tomorrow – my next down time. I was desperate to speak to him and thank him for the gorgeous bouquet of flowers that had arrived for me. Can you believe Lewis sent me 100 red roses? I nearly died! His card was so heartfelt, too.

Naturally, I knew he'd want to speak to me, so

when I rang him the next morning, I was very disappointed his phone was switched off. He knew I would call! If I'm honest I was confused too, and I started panicking. He'd been to see Drake on Valentine's night with some mates. 'He's stayed out! He's with someone,' I kept saying, but everybody in the house told me to shut up and stop being so paranoid.

'Marnie, stop being a complete psycho! He's probably on the Tube!' Sophie rolled her eyes at me. So I sent him a message instead.

It was late afternoon by the time Lewis eventually called me back but, no joke, he sounded *really* weird.

'Alright, darlin'!' he shouted down the phone. He was so over-the-top.

'I'm so glad you called,' I said. 'I was panicking thinking you'd probably taken a girl back to a hotel after Drake and shagged her.'

'Don't be so ridiculous!' he shouted back. He even mentioned he was going to cancel an upcoming skiing trip he had planned with his mates to take me away instead. He said Drake was banging and he'd spent the whole night hanging out with the lads.

'No *sluts* around last night, were there?' I said jokingly.

'No. No sluts . . .'

Can you believe Lewis even started talking dirty to me?

Five days later, I was so excited. Lewis planned to pick me up from the house. I got showered and I made so much effort to look fresh for him. Filming was finished, although I still had green screen to do, but then another weird thing happened. For some unexplained reason, no one was allowed their phones back until I'd finished. 'That's strange,' I kept thinking. Then I got sent to the office directly after I came out of the studio. Sat there in the room were the two executive producers, Rebecca and Claudia. Their faces said it all. It looked like someone had died!

'Marnie, you need to ring your agent,' Rebecca said solemnly. My mind was racing. I was so scared!

'I'm not switching my phone on till you tell me,' I said. But they insisted on me ringing Craig.

'I'm sorry, honey, a video's emerged of Lewis,' he told me.

'What the fuck? What is it?'

'He's in a taxi with two girls. He tried to kiss one, but she pulled away . . .'

My heart was beating. I felt sick. Then the video landed in my inbox. I sat and watched it in silence, trying to take it in. I almost jumped when my phone started ringing and Lewis's name flashed up. I took a deep breath and pretended like nothing had happened.

'I'm ten minutes away. See you soon, babe,' he said.

The lying, cheating scumbag. I hung up, waited for a few minutes then forwarded the video to him.

The minute I got outside, Lewis was standing waiting. He looked as cocky as fuck. 'You're an arsehole. You're a fucking arsehole,' I screamed at him. 'Why were you in taxis with girls on Valentine's night? Where did you go afterwards?'

'I swear to God, I went home.'

'Swear to God. Swear on your family's life!'

'I swear nothing happened!'

'You're a liar!'

Lewis claimed his mates were following in another taxi behind, but within moments he'd let slip they'd all got the train earlier and he'd been left on his own. The minute his story changed, I exploded.

'Fuck off!' I screamed. With that Lewis got in the car and drove off and I carried on to the wrap party in House of Smith. I even kissed one of the house newbies, Sam, that night, although I didn't fancy him. I felt so angry with Lewis, I was gunning for anyone. Given the mindset I was in, I probably shouldn't have gone at all, and I did get absolutely shit-faced.

In the morning, I felt so ashamed. The problem was that in the video Craig had sent me, Lewis didn't actually kiss either of the girls, and I felt I'd behaved ten times worse than him, especially as Nathan had posted a picture of me and Sam on his Snapchat. I was mortified! If Lewis saw that picture I knew he was going to go mental.

I was lying in bed at Mam's with Sophie crying my

eyes out feeling so guilty when Craig emailed me again. This time it was with a link to a video on the *Sun*'s website. Alongside the link he'd written: 'I'm so sorry. I'm here if you need me.'

What the hell? Every muscle in my body didn't want to click on that link, but curiosity was eating me up. The first thing I saw was two girls and Lewis in a cab asking to be dropped at the Double Tree Hilton. Then the film cut to Lewis in bed with one girl on top of him kissing him. Never in my life have I broken down like that over a boy. I could barely breathe, I was so devastated. His lying was worse than his cheating. Only days before he'd been talking dirty *to* me, and now he'd done the dirty *on* me! I started fitting – punching the sofa and screaming and crying. Mam says it was like I was possessed by a demon. Her face turned ashen when she watched the clip because Mam really liked Lewis and had so many hopes for us. But Mam's never been cheated on, so I don't know if she truly understood how I felt.

Afterwards I sent everything to Lewis's mam. She was disgusted with him, but I made it clear I wanted Lewis out of the flat by the time I got back to London. I told him as much when he drunkenly called me.

How could he have been so stupid? He didn't even know those girls. They were from Bristol on a night out in London. They recognised him in the cab queue and invited him in. One of them said in the *Sun* article that she didn't even fancy him, so it was clear he'd been set up. Those girls had played Lewis so badly and the idiot had fallen for it! In some ways, the article hurt me more than the video. One of the girls claimed Lewis had told her he was with me 'just for the money'. That cut me very deeply. The relationship was so real to me. I thought, 'If you're in it for the money, Lewis, you can do one!'

It sounds crazy, I know, but I had this overwhelming need to contact the girls involved, so I did over Instagram. One of them, Amelia, replied instantly. She confessed she was fully clothed in the video and that she and Lewis hadn't had sex. She also said she was sorry. She even told me she'd never wanted to go public with it. Wasn't she forgetting she'd sold the story to a newspaper! Duh! 'Girls like you aren't sorry. You're scum,' I wrote. It's not even funny what happened next, but she messaged me back asking whether she could set me up with her brother as he'd always fancied me. Nice ego boost, but *please*! The bare-faced cheek of the girl! Who tries to shag someone's boyfriend and then wants to set them up with her brother? Total scumsville.

What was lovely was that all my *Geordie Shore* friends left me the most amazing messages. Even Gaz, the biggest fanny rat on the planet, sent me the funniest voice note. He said, 'I can't believe how blatant he is. He doesn't give a fuck. If he's going to do that then just fuck him off!' Then Holly sent me a message saying her heart was breaking for me and I was better off without him. Hannah Elizabeth from *Love Island* dropped me a voice note saying how disgustingly she thought Lewis had behaved. And my favourite was Chloe who posted a video of her farting in the bath. That girl knows exactly how to cheer me up!

A couple of days later, I needed to be back in London to film a new series called *Troll Hunters*, which is all about online abuse. It's probably the last thing I felt like doing but I told myself there was no point weeping into a pillow at home. With or without Lewis, I had to get out and face the world. I even blocked his number on my phone and my WhatsApp, but a friend of his messaged me saying Lewis had fled to Turkey because he was so humiliated and embarrassed by what he'd done. 'Why should I care?' I thought. Then I scrolled through Twitter and saw all the hate he was receiving on social media. I did feel a little sorry for him, and I agreed he could FaceTime me from abroad. It's impossible to explain this, but I had so much anger towards Lewis, yet I still loved him. How mixed up is that? And all the time we were talking, Lewis kept telling me he loved me and how sorry he was.

Of course, all this was before the second bombshell hit. Later that day, another girl messaged me to say that Lewis had picked her up on the beach in Barcelona and taken her back to her hotel room. They'd kissed but not had sex. What the actual fuck? How did Lewis even have time to pull a girl in Barcelona? I didn't understand! But this girl sounded genuine and she was trying to warn me off him. She'd recognised him from all the recent coverage and claimed not to have known he had a girlfriend. Of all the low-down things Lewis had done, Barcelona made me feel more gutted than anything. That holiday was so special to me.

Whatever it took, I had to get the truth out of Lewis and I had my chance when he arrived home. He looked like shit – as if he'd been drunk for days. If I'm honest I was very worried about him. Lewis can go to some dark places in his head. I even told him I thought he was sick and needed help!

Thankfully, we didn't row straight away. Instead, we talked. He said he'd been angry he was alone on Valentine's night and so jealous I was in the *Geordie Shore* house with two of my exes. I did see things from Lewis's point of view, but the bottom line was, these were just excuses. At one point I even climbed on top of him on the sofa, held his head and looked into his eyes.

'Tell me the truth. Was Barcelona true?'

'No. No,' he kept saying.

'Just tell me the truth!' I was thumping at his chest.

I got Lewis's hand, put it on his heart and told him

to swear on his two nephews' lives that he wasn't lying. Lewis loves those little boys. All of a sudden, he went silent and I knew. I just knew.

'You fucking liar,' I screamed. 'You're seriously fucked up!' I grabbed the TV remote and chucked it at his head, but he just lay there and took it!

What I couldn't get my head around was that in Barcelona, Lewis had left our hotel room in the early hours of the morning, gone to the beach while I was asleep and pulled a girl. It was the same night we had the argument over Kyle Walker. But we'd made up! We'd even had sex back at the hotel room! To get back at me, he'd picked up a random, taken her back to her hotel room and kissed her while I was innocently in bed asleep. Now that's not normal, is it?

I can't even explain what happened next without feeling so ashamed, but the day Lewis came back from Turkey, we did end up having sex. He literally broke down in front of me and my heart melted for him. He said he'd been jealous, angry and insecure in Spain and that's what drove him to pull the girl. Whether I believed him or not, I didn't know, but he promised he was going to seek help to sort his head out. Deep down, I loved him. My head was, and still is, a total mess.

Over the next couple of days, I felt so hurt by Lewis that it automatically drew me towards him. Mad, huh? I think now I hadn't really processed what he'd done. As the days wore on, I was beginning to realise that I loved him but I couldn't live with him because I didn't trust him. He'd ruined everything. And it became crystal clear that Lewis had no intention of going into therapy. I went from wanting to give him another chance to wanting him out of my life.

I even contacted a guy in Kent who carried out lie-detector tests. He'd won awards and everything, but Lewis point-blank refused to do one. The final straw was when he strolled in from a night out at eight a.m. and he couldn't even tell me where he'd been.

'We have to finish,' I said to him. 'I can't do this anymore.' Where I got the strength from I don't know, but we still ended up arguing all day. At one point, Lewis was in my car smashing his foot against the windscreen and, in a moment of madness, I tried to escape the car while it was still moving. After that, I insisted Lewis move all his stuff out.

That night I went out to a magazine launch party. I cannot tell you what a relief it was not to have Lewis in my life, even for a few hours. Things had got that bad between us, that I'm sure he felt the same. But his mates from *TOWIE*, Dan Edgar and Tom Pearce, were at the party and the papers ran a story the next day saying I been cosying up with Tom Pearce and disappearing off with him, which wasn't true. There weren't even any pictures!

Lewis must have seen the story, and somehow got

it into his head that I'd kissed one of them. I explained that I hadn't kissed either but I had kissed someone else so because of that he sent me the most awful messages I've ever received in my life. He said he prayed I was dead. He posted loads of mug shots of me looking mortal. He even called me a webbed-foot, big-nosed Geordie cunt! And he said he wanted to get my head and kick it around like a football. How twisted is that? Also, had Lewis suddenly forgotten that he was unfaithful to me? Lewis Bloor was finally showing his true colours . . .

EPILOGUE

What is it with me and boys? I didn't want to finish this book banging on about me and Lewis, but that's where I am in my life. Don't get me wrong, I've done some incredible things since being in *Geordie Shore.* I've met some amazing people and been to some amazing places. I wouldn't change any of it for the world. But Lewis? I guess we'll have to see where that relationship ends up. By the time this book is published we might be history. Or we might be planning our wedding! Either way, I've discovered a lot about myself on the journey. As one of my tattoos says, 'Never a failure, always a lesson'.

And yes, before you ask, me and Lewis have had sex again – after a charity boxing match he won against Heavy D. I even wrote to a friend afterwards saying I'd lost the plot and I should literally cut off my vagina if I slept with Lewis again. Oh well! Been there, done that, worn the T-shirt. And yes, we have argued again. And no, I'm not taking him back. Ask me again tomorrow, though, and I might say the complete opposite!

However messed up things feel at the moment, I still think I'm the luckiest girl in the world. I've got Mam and Eric, me dad, my agent Craig, my mates and all of my *Geordie Shore* family around me. Those people have so much love for me, it's crazy. And sometimes, just sometimes, pain is about discovering what's really important in life.

It's only now that I can begin to appreciate the biggest lessons I've learned. I'm fully aware I'm not the perfect girl and some of my decisions aren't angelic either, but trust me, there's not a single day that I don't think about the choices I've made. It's been a wild rollercoaster and whilst I may not have always behaved in the best manner, I want you all to know that this experience with Lewis has made me see things so clearly. To fall so deeply in love, and for that love to be so disrespected, destroyed me, and it definitely changed me – if anything, it's made me a stronger and better person. I'll never treat anyone how Lewis treated me, and I'll know how to appreciate the good guy when he comes along.

Everything turns out OK in the end, just be true to yourself. And that's what you all should remember: never stop looking up, my darlings.

As for what happens next for me, who knows. You'll just have to wait and see . . .